D1825798

My Father
A HURLING REVOLUTIONARY

Conor Power

Published by

three good boys

First published in 2009 by Three Good Boys Publishing
Ardogeena
Durrus
Co. Cork
Ireland

ISBN 978-0-9563690-0-0

Index compiled by Cover to Cover

Edited by Power Editing

Printed in Ireland by Inspire Design & Print, Skibbereen, County Cork.

Front Photo (also used on page 2) reproduced with kind permission of Examiner Publications

For Mam…

SPONSORS

The O'Flynns of South Coast Transport, Corrin, Fermoy, Co. Cork.

McDonnell Bros., Coolagown, Fermoy, Co. Cork.

Michael Pendergast, New York, USA.

Waterfordmen's GAA Association of New York.

Nemeton TV, An Rinn, Dungarvan, Co. Waterford.

Goalpost Ireland, Tallow, Co. Waterford.

Knockanore Cheese, Knockanore, Co. Waterford.

TABLE OF CONTENTS

PREFACE

Before and during the writing of this book, I spoke to a lot of other people who had written or had attempted to write books. Some of them had not finished their books; some had finished them but had not had them published; some had had them published to some acclaim but didn't sell any; and some had had fantastic success. I discovered that the one factor they all had in common is that they suffered from a severe case of procrastination.

One prominent journalist told me how she had taken a year off to write a book. She got up the first morning and got down a few hundred words. On the third day, realising that she had put herself completely in charge of her own destiny and seeing as it was such a nice sunny day, she took the morning off to enjoy the sunshine. If you're to go by the existentialist philosophy of Jean-Paul Sartre that we are defined by our actions alone, then a month later this lady had ceased to be an author and had instead become a professional dosser.

Fear of finishing the book, the fear that no-one will want to read it and the fear of procrastinating so much that you turn into a dosser and don't write anything – these are the fears that stalk the mind of the writer.

Happily however, I would like to say for the record that I have been nagged into writing this book. I don't need to name the naggers – they know who they are, but I would like to thank them because, without nagging, we might all become dossers and never achieve anything.

CHAPTER 1

STARTING WITH A PHOTOGRAPH

For as long as I can remember, I've been boasting that my father won an All-Ireland medal for Waterford in the 1959 All-Ireland senior hurling final. It became such a running joke in fact that, in introducing me, certain friends would get the business of imparting this background knowledge out of the way as soon as possible – by way of a joke, you see: 'This is Conor… [Hellos and handshakes follow]… His father won an All-Ireland medal for Waterford in 1959. Yes… They beat Kilkenny in the replay.'

Even though it was all in good humour, the whole joke of me ensuring to tell everyone I met about my dad was actually a great and unembarrassing vehicle that actually allowed me to tell everyone about my father. Because I was always as proud as punch of him. Although I had stopped playing hurling at about the age of 14–15, Waterford is a dyed-in-the-skin thoroughbred hurling county. I like to think, in fact, that our small county is to hurling what Holland is to soccer. Like Waterford and its hurling, soccer in Holland is of the highest skill level and they regularly punch above their weight with larger countries around them that have a much bigger pool of players – such as France, Germany, England and Italy. Yet, despite all this, the Dutch have never

won the World Cup, unlike all of their aforementioned neighbours. In a similar way, we the people of the Déise are what you might say mad into our hurling. We can play it skilfully and, for such a small county, we regularly produce a high number of good players. We regularly punch above our weight in this respect, but we don't get much in the way of big trophies. I'm afraid we don't – or at least, not as much as we feel we deserve to get.

All this is to explain why I was always so proud of the 1959 thing. It's because we haven't won it since and people with any knowledge of hurling are always surprised and amazed to meet someone with a physical connection to a Waterford team that actually won an All-Ireland – it's that rare.

Although I'd seen this famous photograph before, it wasn't until I was at least in my late teens that I realised that it was a famous photo. I've since discovered that it is definitely the most famous thing about my father. All those who know of him will be more than familiar with it, but equally many people who know or care nothing about hurling will have seen it. It was taken on June 8th, 1962 in a Munster semi-final match between Cork and Waterford. The photographer was a man named Louis McMonagle and it was entitled 'Hell's Kitchen'. It is a classic action photo and it has appeared in numerous locations around the world – for many who don't know the first thing about hurling, it's as good an introduction as any to its mixture of physical force, danger, speed and pure skill. All of that is encapsulated in this one famous shot.

But pictures can be deceiving: looking at the heroic manner in which my dad appears to rise into the air and snatch the ball out of the sky, leaving the other players tangling on the earth, it all looks like an athlete at the top of his game going on to conquer all in an unstoppable team. But sport is not always a place for fairytales and, in truth, my father was fortunate, at that point, to be picked on the team and to subsequently make it into that photo.

In 1961, more than a year before this picture had been taken, Waterford's All-Ireland winning goalie – 31-year-old Ned Power – was sitting, deep in concentration, waiting patiently to line out in goal against Tipperary. Another team-member, a regular battler with pre-match nerves, noticed what he mistakenly took to be the same pre-match jitters in Ned and offered him a 'tablet' (this was in the good old drug-free days in sport!). The tablet turned out to be a 'downer' and Ned played an uncharacteristically sluggish and unfocused first half making several costly mistakes much to the consternation of the coaching staff. He was taken off at half time and unceremoniously dropped from the panel. His days were over. He 'hadn't it' any more…

Ned could easily have lived out his days in bittersweet memory of his highs with Waterford that petered out in the low of that bizarre drug-coloured 'final' match. Mick Curley, another famous Tallow goalkeeper and himself unlucky not to make the '48 All-Ireland winning team, urged him to 'keep playing, keep making yourself available'. This he did.

A year went by and Ned kept playing and kept positive, a 32-year old has-been waiting for one more chance. A week before this picture was taken he got a phone call from a somewhat reluctant Waterford county board member. They were stuck and he was their last resort. The words they used were 'Ned, would you ever come along on Sunday …we've no-one'. My father's own words were even less complimentary. He said that he 'must have been the best of a bad lot.' So along he came and the months and weeks of pent-up frustration and preparation for this moment launched him into a sparkling display that peaked with that famous leap into the sky, caught magically for eternity.

The Cork man in the photo is recognisable to any hurling fan – particularly if he/she is from Cork because it is none other than the famous Christy Ring, who died a relatively young man at the age of 58. The Waterford defender he's tangled with in manly embrace is Tom Cunningham, while the third Waterford player in the picture is Austin Flynn. All of these players were teetotalling 'Pioneers' and, in the case of the Waterford players, came from the same school – namely Dungarvan Christian Brothers School (CBS) Secondary School. That said, they were never in the same class – my father was the eldest, followed by Tom a year below and Austin a couple of more years below Tom.

The day after the match, my dad was back at his place of work – Scoil Mhuire National School in Tallow, County Waterford, where he was principal. At 11 o'clock, a pupil named John McDonnell came up to him as he was walking by the school building with his colleague Mrs Abbie Ahern. John brought him the paper and it was then that my father saw the famous shot for the first time. My dad's reaction was minimal. He was never interested in glorification of any one player in a team or even in the glorification of any one team from a place, and particularly so if it was he who was the centre of attention. John's memory of my father's reaction was that it was 'not a lot… the same as when anyone said anything good about him or of a very high proportion. He'd bring it down to a more ordinary level altogether.'

After playing hurling at the highest level for Waterford during their most golden era, my father led a life which was to be dominated by GAA. He was a husband and a father of six and he led his own little revolution around the country which was to touch the lives of many people, working at the grass roots: at the more ordinary level of things.

CHAPTER 2

MY FATHER, THE TEACHER

My dad taught me in school. He also taught all of my brothers, but not my sisters – they both went to the girls' school in Tallow, where my mother taught. This was an ever-so-slightly odd experience because ideally being a teacher means that you will have empathy for your students but you must also maintain a professional distance. It needn't necessarily present any problems that your teacher is also your parent, but it's still a strange enough situation to find yourself in. It is probably comparable to running a multinational business and having, say, your mother as the chief financial officer. That would be rather strange, although my mother probably would have made a good financial officer now that I think of it.

Anyway, my dad was the principal of our local St Mary's Primary School, Tallow (or Scoil Mhuire, Tulach an Iarainn, to give its more official Irish title) since long before I was born, which meant that he taught 5th and 6th class. So I had a lot of school-hours to clock up before I worked my way up to his classroom. When I was in the lower classes, I used to get the very occasional glimpse of what my father the teacher was all about. He was partly a stranger to me in the routine yet foreign-structured environment of the primary school. At school, he was always that bit louder and more animated than he was at home. He didn't sit reading the newspaper at school (which was a regular indulgence at home), for example. He was always sharp and alert in the classroom; a more highly tuned, focused and less tolerant version of the guy I was familiar with from home.

It was always interesting to me too the manner in which the children in school reacted to him. They all addressed him as 'Sir' or 'Mr Power'. In fact, as former pupil and Tallow GAA stalwart John McDonnell pointed out to me, there are still those that referred to my father as Mr Power, long after passing into adulthood. They seemed more respectful of him than I was and more fearful of crossing him, something which made me wonder. I felt like letting them know that there was really nothing to fear from him, that it was just Dad acting all strict and important. He used to make them laugh too, with many of the gags that I was familiar with from the home version of Ned Power. Only, in class, his delivery was turned up a few octaves to a near-manic level of performance.

I have a hazy memory of being sent on an errand by my teacher in 2nd class to my dad's 5th & 6th class next door and seeing my father in action as a teacher for the first time. It's an intimidating enough experience as a 7-year-old walking into a class full of 12- and 13-year-olds. But to find your father amongst them, poking slight fun at your presence and making them laugh is even stranger. I was probably a little envious of those older children who were all enjoying my father's humour, only they seemed to find him even funnier than I did, and I was relieved to have my own dad back at home that evening. I understood then that the transformation wasn't permanent – that he went from home-dad to school-dad and back again every day.

By the time I got to become one of my father's pupils, I had already seen plenty of instances of him as a teacher to know roughly what to expect. He did keep it all simple and offered me no special treatment above the others, even though I was his son. Often, in fact, it was harder for people on the outside looking in to be able to make sense of this perceived dilemma than it was for us. Once when Seán was in 6th class with his father as his teacher, my dad had to give him a dressing down in front of the other children for some transgression. As the rest of the class looked on with a fascinated mixture of shock and curiosity, one of Seán's classmates said in disbelief 'Sure, he's his father!' looking from father to son and back.

My father used a lot of similar philosophies both in teaching and in sport. About sport, he always saw it as not only something in which you could build character but also something where your character was revealed for its true self. If you were the sort of person who would have a nasty dig – a cheap shot – at someone on the field of play, then you were likely to do the same in your dealings with people in life in general.

The team was always more important than any one individual and it was through the team that redemption was to be found and character was to be built. This, I think, was at the heart of his philosophy. It was, I believe, a very socialist form of thinking and one which is now almost completely lacking in the value-less and amoral mess that passes for political leadership in our Republic at the present time of writing.

So, in teaching too, he wanted no more than for someone to do their level best in anything they did. You can do no more than that. You can't take a shot from your left side? Then just pass it to someone who can. You don't know the Irish word for orange? Then describe it as a mixture of red and yellow. The importance of the team, of inclusiveness and of the mutual benefit in everyone working towards a common purpose was paramount in his whole approach to teaching. As far as he was concerned, the classroom was a team making a journey all together from September of one year to June of the next. If everybody did their level best and approached the work to be done with honesty, then we would all get along well and we would all get the best results possible.

My older sister Patricia is the only one of my siblings (at the time of writing at least) who has followed in both his and my mother's footsteps of becoming a primary school teacher and she, like my father, adopts the same team approach when it comes to teaching.

His discipline was strong because he knew how to 'work the crowd' and he had what the New York Police Department might call a 'zero tolerance level' with regard to anyone stepping out of line. Corporal punishment was part of the education process during my school days and my dad administered it only when it was deemed necessary, which was very rarely.

I came across a former pupil of my father's once in a pub in Rathmines, Dublin. It was the late 1980s and I was a student in our capital city when my flatmates and I decided to go around the corner to the 'Lower Deck'. This pub was famous at the time as its resident Sunday-morning novelty act consisted of a lady with an outsized bosom who went under the stage name 'Toni the Exotic Dancer'. Leaving that irrelevancy aside (it was a Thursday night anyway), I spotted Killian

Herlihy at the bar; he was a friend of my older brother Seán and he was in the company of another Tallow man. His name will remain anonymous – I've actually forgotten it since and even Killian himself couldn't remember the incident when I mentioned it to him at Dad's funeral – but he was well oiled and wavering by the time we got talking to him. He spent the rest of the evening repeating the following series of slurred sentences several times through half-closed eyes:

'Are you Ned Power's son? Jaysus! I knew your father well! He was a great man. He was hard, but he was fair. He'd hit you, alright, if he had to. I got hit by him once or twice, but I deserved it. There'll be a monument to that man! You mark my words!'

Those last words, which were repeated to me that night on possibly 20 separate occasions and which have been repeated countless times since in mimicry, were to become a true prophecy when a monument was erected to him in 2004 at the GAA field in Tallow, now renamed 'Páirc Éamonn de Paor'.

CHAPTER 3

GROWING UP IN DUNGARVAN

I parked the car on the hill of St Brigid's Terrace and looked around. To my left was a row of terraced houses. Down near the end I saw the house with its brown door and the garden in front, the last but one. This was the house I knew growing up as Granny Power's. It was often dark inside – the kitchen lit by a rear window through which daylight had difficulty penetrating as it struggled past tightly packed neighbouring houses, garden walls and a net curtain.

But Granny and my dad's sister Eileen always had a warm welcome. Dad's mother was as jolly as Santa Claus himself and very easy to make laugh. Questions after our well being were often punctuated with laughter, no matter how we responded. My father, looking on, would say something else to make his mother laugh – usually an impersonation of some local character. We would hang around impatiently while the mysterious adult conversations went off on their own merry tangent, awaiting the inevitable arrival of treats. They were never brought out straight away. As a young boy of seven or eight, I could not, for the life of me, understand why they didn't get the entire thing over and done with as soon as possible, but I suppose they got too much pleasure by indulging in the whole ceremony of allowing the momentum build up sufficiently to the point where the question would be asked 'I suppose you'd hate a treat, would ye?' at which point my Dad would join in, saying something like 'Oh, they hate biscuits.'

I remember always feeling worried that Dad would scupper the opportunity altogether and was always nervous that, some day, Granny would actually take him at his word and withdraw the offer. In any case, that never happened. I remember biding my time going out the back yard, which was mysterious to me at the time, with its neighbours right next door and the gate at the end which led somewhere else.

Very possibly the last time I visited my grandmother was when I was in my mid-to-late teens. I had cycled all the way from Tallow to Dungarvan by bike. It was a distance of about 32 km. I wasn't used to it and I was fairly exhausted from the effort. She was suffering a form of senility towards the end of her life and she kept asking me the same question every few minutes: 'It's lovely to see you. How did you get here?' When I told her that I cycled all the way, she threw her head back laughing. After another few minutes, she'd ask the question all over again and get the same thrill out of the answer all over again.

I didn't know it until more than a year after his death, but I was repeating a journey that had often been undertaken by my father when he was a young single teacher in Tallow. His youngest brother Brendan told me that when they were in their early twenties, they both shared digs in Tallow, where my father was principal in the local boys' school. Brendan was teaching there too. Every weekend they would make the journey home to Dungarvan, with my dad often using the bike to do it.

'Your father was always keeping fit,' Brendan explained to me, adding that he himself wouldn't ordinarily take on such a long journey. As was common amongst fit men in 1950s' Ireland, my father smoked cigarettes and would typically be seen atop his bike wearing a cap, with a fag dangling from his lips. He was a smoker in a time when cigarette companies advertised in an as-yet unrestricted manner, when reports linking smoking to lung cancer were suppressed and when smoking was regarded as just a bit of good old-fashioned fun. I never knew him as a smoker – he had managed to stop before I was aware of it – but he was an enthusiastic consumer of tobacco back then, in the early half of the 1950s.

But what, I wondered, was the Power household like? I was anxious to get to know the dynamics of the large family of seven children and where my father fitted in.

First of all, there were those seven children in all. Not a large family at the time by any stretch of the imagination, at first they all lived in a house on Stephen Street, off the main O'Connell Street in Dungarvan. They vacated just a few hundred metres south to a house on St Brigid's Terrace in the town. Brendan still has memories of the house as being 'nice and homely'.

'I was four at the time... making an educated guess,' says Brendan, recalling the big move 60-odd years later in the kitchen of his home in Bandon. Interestingly, he remembers it as being a move to a bigger house, which doesn't tally with what his siblings Seán and Mary say, but in the excited mind of a four-year-old boy, somewhere new is always going to feel bigger and better.

The Powers of St Brigid's Terrace and formerly of Stephen Street, Dungarvan, County Waterford consisted of: Pat (born 1925, died 2008), Ned (born 1929, died 2007), Kitty (born 1932, died 2006), Seán (born 1934), Eileen (born 1935), Mary (born 1936) and Brendan (born 1937). There was also another son David who was born between Dad and Kitty but who didn't survive.

When they were making their move to new accommodation in 1941, the world was engaged in a series of acts of slaughter known as the Second World War. Ireland had managed to remain neutral, but as the war continued, more and more signs were becoming evident that the country could not remain completely untouched and was in an increasing state of readiness for whoever was going to attack them.

All over the countryside, defensive pill-boxes were set up with armed soldiers manning them. Signposts were taken down in order to create maximum confusion for any invading forces. (There are tourists today who maintain that a similar policy still exists.) Spies were employed by the fledgling Free State of Ireland in order to literally keep the ears and eyes of the Republic to the ground, providing the occasional fortunate individual with a budget for socialising in somewhat straightened times. Most importantly of all, food and basic commodities such as coal were rationed.

'People say that they were tough times, but they weren't,' so said my uncle Seán, an artist and former primary school teacher, who grew up in the same house as my father, his brother. He is the only one of the four brothers who has actually stayed in the Dungarvan area and his house in Abbeyside is one that I have very fond memories of. I stayed there a few times as a child. It was, and still is, a large and fantastic old house, full of character, creaks and eccentricities, surrounded by mature gardens full of dark and mysterious corners, a pond from which live frogs emerged in large numbers at a certain time of year, a tall hedge through which you passed to gain access to the field, at the end of which there was the strand.

Now, on this sunny spring day in 2009 listening to my uncle recall his childhood, it feels exactly as it did when I was a boy, except that the field between the house and the sea is now an estate of new houses. 'Everything was better then,' he continues. 'The food was better, the air was cleaner. We lived in a country where vandalism was non-existent… If I was staying in my auntie's in the countryside, there was only very rarely a sound from the road, there was no hum of a fridge, no television, no central heating. There was a silence in that world which can't exist any more. There was no plumbing to be done, there were no phone or electricity bills to worry about. You got water from the well, you went outside to get timber for the fire and you had a magical world of shadows at night. There was literally nothing to go wrong.'

During the Emergency (the Irish word for World War II), John Power – the father of the family and my grandfather – was called upon to serve his country and he spent four years stationed in barracks in Cork. My father was the second eldest in the family, but his older brother Pat had gone to join the Christian Brothers at the tender age of 14 (from where he was to emerge as an adult at the age of 25). This left my father in a position of father-figure for much of the time. By all accounts, it was one in which he thrived.

'Your father was very domesticated,' said Brendan. 'He was great for breaking blocks or bringing in coal – that sort of thing.' The early departure of the eldest in the family to pursue a monastic life also meant, in the words of Brendan, that 'he never to know us and we never got to know him.'

Eileen also remembers my father as someone who inherited a paternal role that he accepted and excelled in: 'Your grandfather started the garden, and then your father took it over… He was very intent on it – he used to grow cabbage, peas, everything. We used to get pig manure from Dwyers down the street from us.' She also remembers my father cooking meals when it was necessary, as it was on one occasion when their mother was ill in hospital. 'And after doing the cooking, washing and everything, he used to go into the front room and study. He was housekeeper and doctor.'

Brendan, as the youngest in the family, readily admits to getting special treatment as such, but they all remember my father as very kind-hearted and entertaining from a very young age. 'He was always full of stories,' says Brendan, 'no matter where he had been and he always had the mimicry to give you the full picture.'

This was, it seems, in sharp contrast to his own father. I never met John Power – he had died nine years before I was born – but it appears that he was a very serious man; a man for whom his children had great respect but who was not the jocular sort. 'He had no time for anything that was fake or plastic,' Seán says of his father, 'On St Patrick's Day, for example, he would never stand for wearing manufactured badges – shamrock was what you wore! Everything was neat and regimental with him.' The amusing, entertaining side seemed to come much more from his mother's side, a lady that Brendan describes as 'very entertaining and very shrewd. She always got to the point. She'd know what you have said before you realised it yourself.'

John was a man of intellectual pursuits. When he was in Cork, he would attend the opera. He taught himself to read music and to play the violin, using the blank side of an oatmeal box on which to write out his compositions. His efforts weren't best appreciated at the time, however. His children would regard fiddle-playing as an old-fashioned 'tinkers' trade'.

The hanging-out place and the meeting place for children in Dungarvan at that time was 'Quann's'. This was a large field that belonged to a family named Quann and which was situated on the coast on a vacant site which is now rather fittingly occupied by a sports centre. This was where youngsters spent their time and this was where the budding GAA star would hit his first sliotar.

'We spent a lot of time there,' says Seán. 'We made our own sliotar. I've forgotten how it was made but we had to make one – this was during the war, you see. We used to play 'score and three', where one person went into goal and then when you scored three goals, you got a chance to go in.'

If a child wasn't at home, then he was to be found at Quann's. Where is so-and-so? He's down at Quann's. Let's all go down to Quann's. Are you coming to Quann's?

My father's best friend growing up in Dungarvan was a boy called Patsy Burke. He was also good friends with Patsy's brother Michael, but my father and Patsy were bosom buddies, spending much of their youth playing ball of one sort or another at Quann's, Dad being the most keen on sports. My mother often quotes Patsy Burke as an adult saying to my Dad: 'Jesus, Power, it's no good going for a walk with you because as soon as you see any kind of a ball, you're off after it!' The Burkes had a grocery shop and through this connection, my father was fortunate enough to have a rare supply line of occasional goodies, which, according to Eileen, he was always prepared to share with his siblings when he got home.

Just where my father's love of sport came from, I'm not so sure. There is simply no history of any of my father's ancestors or relatives being interested in sport. Although Seán was keen on hurling for a time in his youth, he never pursued it and in any case, he did not have the 24-hour passion that my father seemed to have for sport from early childhood. Whether it was kicking a ball against the door of the family home with both feet, keeping it going for hours or walloping a makeshift emergency-ration sliotar with Patsy Burke or Matty Fitzgerald down at Quann's (which, apparently, was also an excellent venue for developing your skills at keeping the ball low, because if you hit it too high, you lost your ball to the Atlantic Ocean), his interest in sport was as single-minded as it was unique amongst the members of his extended family.

Seán remembers his obsession with sport extending to listening to the results of the soccer matches on the radio: 'To me, it didn't make any sense at all because the name of the guy who had the ball was all that was mentioned in the commentary… Nobody said anything else at all! It was boring – the complete opposite to Micheál Ó Hehir. And he'd listen intently to this because he loved all sport.'

A lot of his love of hurling was nurtured and developed while at secondary school. At the CBS, Brother Murray had a very positive effect on him, both from the educational point of view as well as the hurling one. In any case, my father seems to have always been a conscientious pupil – his academic discipline and prowess seemingly a reflection of his white-shirted neatness and organisation at home – from primary through secondary school. One schoolmate from primary school and secondary school was Davy Hourigan: 'There were about 36 or 37 of them in that class,' he says, 'and about half of them went onto secondary school and it ended up being nine going on to complete the Leaving Cert.

'Ned was a great fella in school. He had great life in him – he was a pleasant, bubbly type of guy. He was a very good student, very diligent and he was one who meant to get on. We had a good hurling team in the Christian Brothers and he was a good hurler. Of course, we only knew him as an outfield hurler then when he used to play in the half-forward line.'

Davy also pointed out to me that although our new Republic was aspiring to offer free education for all its citizens, a proper education was still the preserve of the better off except where the Christian Brothers stepped in to provide education that was as close as possible to free. One pound per term, according to Davy, was all that was asked by way of a fee (a very modest amount even in those times) and 'they didn't ask for it again if they didn't get it.'

My Dad never forgot the education that he received from the Christian Brothers and the powerful spiritual and sporting training that he also received from them. I believe that these years had a profound and positive influence on the paths he chose in later life. He acknowledged a lot of this in a piece that he wrote in the *Dungarvan Leader* in April 1996 in which he lamented the disappearance of the Christian Brothers from Irish life:

> This saddens me because I'm a Christian Brothers' product and retain many happy memories of the Brothers of my native Dungarvan, a school which was among the first to be established and from which the order was forced to withdraw a few short years ago. They dominated the educational scene down through those intervening years, such a significant period of our history and their influence on our careers was incalculable… I never forget the Brothers. Whatever I am or whatever I have achieved is due mainly, after my parents, to the wholesome Catholic Irish influence of the Brothers.

Another pal in secondary school who completed the Leaving Certificate the same year as my father was Rory Wyley. When I caught up with Rory, he had already cycled 55 kilometres that day and had recently returned from a trip to South America with his cycling club companions, where he had suffered a fractured pelvis as a result of a fall from a bike. He told me that he used to sit beside Davy Hourigan for the inspiration that he offered in the field of maths. He also told me a lot about cycling. Oh, and that my father was a great sportsman in school and a conscientious student.

The Powers appear to have had a happy upbringing in Dungarvan, but if there was one place they liked being even better it was at their Auntie Bridie's in Affane – a quiet townland between Cappoquin and Dungarvan. Their aunt was married but did not have any children of her own, so she lavished attention on her nephews and nieces from the town. Brendan described it as 'an oasis', where there would sometimes be as many as six of the Dungarvan gang accommodated under their aunt's roof. My dad's sister Mary loved going to Bridie's and described the place as 'wonderful'. On the evening they had to go back home from Affane, there would be a family rosary. Mary remembers trying to get through her prayers with a big lump in her throat from the heartbreak of leaving behind the haven of Auntie Bridie's.

Here, my father was introduced to the sport of hunting for rabbits by Bridie's husband Jerry (a 'nice quiet man who was happy going hunting and going to matches', according to Brendan). Together with Mick Purcell, they used the ferreting technique of flushing out the unfortunate bunnies, which consisted of sending a mean ferret down one hole and then waiting with a net at the other where the rabbit would be expected to attempt escape from the murderous ferret. One important detail was to make sure to deny the ferret the pleasure of getting a hold of the rabbit – an element of the plan that didn't always come off as hoped. My dad enjoyed it all right, although it was his brother Seán who continued pursuing animals and dispatching them to their maker through his adult life.

CHAPTER 4

MY FATHER, THE ACTOR

A little over a year after my father's death, a good friend of mine Donnchadh O'Leary rang me at my home in Durrus. He was ringing live from a public auction in Lismore and was standing in front of a vintage poster from circa 1950 that he was offering to buy on my behalf. The poster announced in tall bold letters that a play was to be held at the Town Hall in Youghal on 'Sunday Next, January 27th, at 8.30 p.m.' The play was entitled *Crime Comes to Ballyconneen* and was due to show for one night only. Rather tantalisingly, the poster announced that 'This Play reveals something entirely new in Amateur Theatricals and should NOT BE MISSED'. The players were from Tallow Tennis Club Dramatic Group and top of the list of the seven actors and actresses was one Ned Power NT. After establishing that the cost of the poster would be in the region of around €40, I gave instructions to my bidder not to let it go.

I never managed to get to see my father in a play, but from the time he arrived in Tallow, he got into acting in a big way, joining the Tallow Tennis Club players along with others, including his long-time pal Connie Ryan. Connie came from a long line of singers and was a fairly decent tenor himself. In fact, he and my dad had made a pact that one would perform at the other's funeral – depending on who died first, of course – with my father opting for a speech from the pulpit, while Connie would sing 'Panis Angelicus'. He was true to his word at my dad's funeral when the octogenarian sang a powerful version of 'Panus' to a packed house. Sadly, Connie passed away himself before I could talk to him at length about the height of my dad's acting career, although he did tell me that he remembered *Crime Comes to Ballyconneen* as one of the better plays they did and was surprised never to have heard of the play again since.

By all accounts, my dad was a terrific actor, particularly in a 'character' role – he had a great talent for mimicry. I imagine too that he would have approached any such role with his usual meticulousness.

Ever before my mam and my dad had become the productive 'item' that they were destined to become, my mother went to see a play from the tennis drama group called *Autumn Fire* – a melodramatic tragedy written by T.C. Murray involving an uncomfortable love triangle between a son, his stepmother and his sickly, widowed father. My mother only knew my dad to see or say hello to at that point, but his performance and his make-up were so perfect that when her friend Eileen Cotter told her who it was, she wouldn't believe it was the young, sporty twenty-something teacher that was playing the part of the old man.

Drama is a time-consuming activity and he never got involved in it again to the degree that he had in his younger years. He did have some notable character roles, for which he received great praise. Even as late as 1994 when he was 65, he received a special award from the judging committee for a part in a play that involved just one line. Having come full circle from his early acting days, my father found himself again playing a wealthy old man, this time being presented by a matchmaker to a young potential wife. After listening to my dad read over his line a few times, my mother advised him to take his cameo appearance as slowly as possible and to wait until he was certain that the audience was listening before delivering the words.

When it came to the performance on the night, with impeccable timing as ever, my father adopted the suitable expression, looked the potential wife up and down for a moment, looked out over the audience and, just when they were ready to burst into giggles, uttered the line: 'I'd nearly say… I'd nearly say she's been saddled before!' The laugh was the biggest of the night and brought the house down.

CHAPTER 5

A TEACHER IN TRAINING

In 1947, my father went to teacher training at St Patrick's Training College (St Pat's), Drumcondra, Dublin. The same institution is there today, only now it's known under the slightly different name of St Patrick's College of Education. It's located in the heart of 'Celtic Tiger Years' Taoiseach Bertie Ahern's constituency. It's only up the road from where Bertie's clinic was and within walking distance of some of his more popular watering holes, where he was (and presumably still is, as I write) wont to socialise with his mates while quaffing pints of Bass.

Free third-level education was the stuff of fantasy in the fledgling Republic, so my father was one of the few in the country at the time that was able to pursue an education. Many didn't and more still emigrated. Our country has a very strong emigration 'habit' that started in earnest in the famine times which were at their height exactly 100 years earlier. In fact, the Powers were very unusual in that I had only one relative on that side living overseas (dad's sister Kitty had emigrated as far as Wales). That's a rare enough thing in Ireland. And on my mother's side, there was only one second cousin that emigrated to Australia. Everyone else remained in Ireland. It's something to be proud of, I reckon, because I think it's quite an achievement for those times. Nowadays, moving abroad for work isn't usually necessary and even it you do, travel is far cheaper so you can pop back home whenever you want. Back then, you left and that was pretty much it, even if it was only as far as Britain.

At the time, there was a student loan scheme of the sort that the current administration has been looking into in recent years. If you applied for certain courses (including primary teacher training), then you were able to avail of this loan scheme. The money would be paid back from earnings over the following three years.

Dad left behind the house on St Brigid's Terrace in Dungarvan where he had been the stand-in patriarch, market gardener and fetcher of fuel for the fire, amongst many other things. He arrived for the first time in his life in the capital city at the age of 17, armed with an overall honours mark in his Leaving Certificate.

In college, he was to continue his interest in GAA games, becoming an active member of the college team Erin's Hope, as RTE commentator Micheál Ó Muircheartaigh remembers:

'He was a senior student and I was a junior. I remember him – he was the football goalkeeper for the college team. It was unusual to have a Waterford footballer, you know. There was another Waterford man who played for the college and for Waterford as well named Tom McHugh, who was in the same year as your father.

'Ned was a very good football goalkeeper and it was an exceptionally good team. Seán Purcell of Galway – a member of the team of the millennium – would have been on it, as well as John-Joe Sheehan of Kerry. He won two All-Irelands as centre-forward in 1953 and 1955. And there was another very good player in Ned Lyons: A Meath man, he won a junior All-Ireland medal with Dublin. So there were lots of good players on the team.'

They were good enough to beat the mighty St Vincent's, who had recently been crowned Dublin senior champions for the first time in their history (a title that they were to dominate, winning it almost every year until the late 1970s).

'It was a big surprise when they beat them in a league game… Ned was as good as anyone on it,' remembers Micheál.

He was playing football in fact, because there was no hurling team in the college at that time, even though they do have a good hurling team today. In any case, my dad was playing more football than anything else at the time. Another man who was in the college at the time was the Waterford hurler Johnny O'Connor, who won a senior hurling All-Ireland medal in 1948, playing at midfield when they beat Dublin.

O'Connor and my father had also been classmates in the CBS in Dungarvan.

'I used to play hurling with UCD [University College Dublin],' says Johnny, whose rapid speech and lively demeanour over the phone belied his advanced years. 'I didn't bother much with the football, even though Seán Purcell and I used to train together. Seán was one of the "terrible twins" from Galway!'

Micheál spoke fondly of my father as a very popular and sociable student: 'Ned was the sort of person, I think, that everyone felt they knew,' says Micheál of his memories of my dad's presence around the institution. 'He was a very sociable type of person; he had a word with everyone and I think that he was that way all his life. He was anxious to talk to people, and to listen to people, which is just as important. Even then, you'd know that he was a good community type of person.

'Some people would go through the college without people knowing them well or conversing much with them, but Ned would be the opposite, that at some stage, he'd be talking to everyone.'

This sounds very much like the sort of man I knew as a father – talking to everyone, whether he was being stopped by acquaintances who wanted a word with him or he was the one doing the stopping. As I knew him growing up, however, Dad was already a very well-known and respected personality. Maybe stopping and talking to people was always a habit of his. Maybe he was the sort of person whom people sought out because he always had something interesting to say. This is the sort of image I've always had of him and what Micheál said seemed to back that up.

Johnny O'Connor gave me a slightly different slant, however, when it came to the social life of my father:

'Ned was very quiet,' said Johnny to me. 'He usen't come out to the dances as much as we did. He was sensible in that respect.'

While they might have moved in slightly different circles socially, they did spend a lot of time training together, along with Seán Purcell. Before and after training, the two Dungarvan men would spend a lot of time chatting and walking around the grounds together.

By necessity, socialising at that time in a third-level institute such as St Pat's did not involve spending large amounts of money or consuming significant quantities of alcohol. Even Johnny O'Connor's weekly forays into the dances on Parnell Square were affordable because of half-price concessions to St Pat's students, whilst my dad would be more inclined to go and see a film in the cinema across the road. I asked Micheál if it was unusual to be a member of the Pioneer Association at that time: 'I would say that everyone in the college was a Pioneer... until you were 18 at least, and a bit beyond it.'

The local 'Cat & Cage' pub across the road from the entrance to the college was, he says 'totally out of bounds'. This, it seems, was more on a nod-and-wink basis than by way of official declaration on the part of the college authorities. Some students would visit occasionally for a pint or two if they had the price of a drink.

'I found it funny, on the odd occasion, I've launched "Seachtain na nGaeilge" and it was launched from the Cat & Cage because the pub was sponsoring the week. So it's a complete turn of the wheel now. There is no way that An Cumann Gaelach or any organisation like that would go near the place. There are different times now.'

Times were very different. My uncle Seán, who was also trained at the same institution, put it even more bluntly – 'They trained you like you'd train a donkey,' he said of the strict Catholic-run regime that operated in the college. It must be remembered that St Pat's then was a purely Catholic institution whose job it was to train Catholic men and women to become primary school teachers of Catholic children. For the Protestant minority, there was another separate system.

And so, in 1949 my father emerged from St Pat's a qualified teacher looking for a job. After a couple of substitute jobs, he was to get a permanent position in a school in Tallow one year later.

CHAPTER 6

MY FATHER, THE SUN WORSHIPPER

For all of his life, my father was a devoted Catholic, but there is a case to be made that he worshipped the sun almost as much as his beloved faith.

With an almost feline persistence, Dad was adept and single-minded at seeking out the warmth of the sun and soaking up its energy while it was there. He was possibly the worst possible example of how not to handle the sun. My mother is still amazed that he never got skin cancer from the days that she could see his forehead 'literally boiling' from hours and hours of over-exposure to the harmful rays of the sun (rays in which he could see no harm whatsoever).

He would not hear of closing the blinds or the curtains of an evening when the sun would be shining directly in our eyes, preventing us from seeing our dinner or even knowing who we were and what we were doing. No, he would say. We're lucky to have this marvellous sunshine and, God knows, we don't get a lot of it in this wonderful country of ours, so we should be thankful and enjoy it while it's shining. I would then squint at the indiscernible silhouette of my father and resume eating my tea (in our house, dinner was in the middle of the day and tea was the meal at evening time) in the unrelenting glare and warmth of the evening sun, whose rarity I found harder to appreciate than my dad did.

His brother Brendan tells me that my dad always behaved like this when it came to sunshine. One of his many abiding memories of Ned is of him in his classic pose, sitting in the sun and reading a newspaper. My father sitting in the sun reading a newspaper is a scene that has been played out in many places and points in his life. I can see him in the extended kitchen of our family home in Tallow, sitting in the car at the beach – an excellent place to take a moment to catch up with the paper and really warm up before heading home again – sitting outside the cottage we'd rented for a memorably sunny holiday on the Dunquin Peninsula in Kerry in 1983.

He always bought a regular batch of newspapers that he would read from cover to cover. When I was growing up, it was the *Cork Examiner* (now the *Irish Examiner*), the *Irish Press* (now defunct) and, once a week, the *Irish Independent*. The latter was a paper he didn't particularly like for its somewhat Fine-Gael heritage and his own father used to refer to it as 'The English Independent'. My mother was always battling with him over the huge volume of papers that came into the house, but until very late in life, my dad was unwavering on this point.

When he got the chance to go abroad and appreciate some serious-level sunshine in countries with warmer climates than ours, it didn't seem to turn him off his sun worship at all. In the pictures of him in New York in 1960 on his post-All-Ireland trip, he's the one with the sleeves rolled up and the top shirt buttons opened. And he loved the warmth of the sunshine in France when my parents first went there together back in 1984.

The sea and the sun were equally adored by my dad. He was never much of a swimmer, my uncle Seán once joked. Having witnessed his unique and laborious style on several occasions, I wouldn't be inclined to argue otherwise. Although he enjoyed it, when swimming he looked like someone who was doing it reluctantly – a child being forced to take his cod liver oil.

We had a set of unique homemade 'changing towels' that my mother had manufactured from regular-type beach towels. There was one which was like a large smock, so that you could pop it over you and then change discreetly into your swimming togs without the added worry of, say, an incident of the towel falling to the ground or a gust of wind causing an unwanted and revelatory 'split'. There were also at least two large un-stylish multi-coloured bath robes in the same vein and it was one of these – the yellow one – that my dad usually went for when changing on the beach.

On one occasion at Red Barn Strand Bay near Youghal (which was one of the many beaches within a half-hour drive of Tallow that we used to frequent on fine summer days), Dad was having a slightly difficult time of it while trying to change out of his swimming togs beside the car, which was parked in the car park overlooking the strand.

Between them, the large yellow robe and the car were offering a maximum level of coverage and comfort. He noticed, at that point, that someone had left the radio on in the car. Naturally, he was concerned that the battery might run down so, mumbling something impatiently like 'What eejit left the radio on?', he reached his hand through the open window and switched it off. But something was not right. The button on the radio didn't feel the way it normally did. In fact, the radio looked different, as did the seats of the car and everything else of the interior. With his fingers still holding the button that had switched off the radio, it suddenly dawned on him that this was not his car at all. He turned his head to see a startled and unfamiliar lady sitting in the driver's seat. She is probably still wondering why this middle-aged man dressed only in a yellow home-made bath robe had reached his hand into her car and switched off the radio she had been quietly listening to.

CHAPTER 7

COMING TO TALLOW

After saying goodbye to St Patrick's Training College in Drumcondra, my father got a position in the Bishop Foley National School on Station Road in Carlow. Here he was to stay a total of 10 months before getting a job in his native county in Tallow.

The image I have of Tallow then is like something out of a Wild West movie. Only I imagine it not as a bustling Wild West town – the lone gunslinger coming into town walking past saloons from which emanates boisterous piano music and fights spilling into the street, stepping over sleeping cowboys and brushing aside painted ladies.

No, the Tallow I imagine in 1950 would probably have been more like the sort of quiet place that Shane himself might have walked through and through which large balls of tumbleweed would have blown.

But that's only because, like all sons, I have a tendency to cast my father in the role of the hero. The reality was somewhat different. This was a typical small town in rural Ireland. Tallow is located at the very western end of County Waterford and as soon as you leave the town on the western side of it, you're in County Cork. So although it's very close to County Cork, it's not in County Cork. That might seem like a very obvious point to some, but it's worth underlining all the same. Because Tallow is not in County Cork. At all.

Tallow is classed as a small town, although there are some from outside of it who would class it as a village. Surrounding it are Lismore (a slightly larger town with a more prestigious past), Ballyduff (classed as a village) and the more rural parishes of Knockanore, Kilwatermoy and Glendine (collectively known under the banner of 'The Shamrocks'). All of these are roughly equidistant from one another and all are in County Waterford, so in GAA terms, the rivalry is intense.

Having just got through the 'Emergency' years, with rations still in force, there was a cautious optimism in the nation as we headed into a new decade. More than twenty years after independence, Ireland had only been declared a republic before the eyes of the world just two years beforehand and it was only in July of 1950 that Britain sent its first ambassador to Dublin.

Interestingly enough, it was in that same year that British prime minister Winston Churchill proposed the establishment of a European army at a European consultative assembly in Strasbourg (seven years before the Treaty of Rome) – an idea which was voted down by representatives of the new Irish Republic. It was the year of the death of author and playwright George Bernard Shaw and the birth of author and film director Neil Jordan. It was, many people then must have hoped, the finish of something old and unwanted and the beginnings of… God knows what, but something exciting in any case.

Few would have predicted that, economically speaking, our fortunes were to go from bad to worse in the 1950s, whilst an unprecedented economic boom would flourish in Britain and across Western Europe. But few would have also predicted that this new 20-year-old teacher – a stranger from Dungarvan with family roots in the east of the county – was to have such a lasting impact on the history of the town.

In the beginning, he was simply the teacher. Without any friends in Tallow, he got himself involved, not with the local GAA (as he was still playing football and hurling with Dungarvan) but with the local Macra na Feirme, the tennis club and its dramatic society. One of the first people he got to know well was local butcher Connie Ryan. Connie sadly passed away during the course of writing this book and before I had an opportunity to conduct a face-to-face interview with him about him and my dad. But, before he died, I did speak to him briefly on the phone about my dad's early years in Tallow.

'We struck up a great relationship straight away,' remembered Connie. 'We had a lot in common. We were involved in a lot of things, but tennis was the main one. I wouldn't have had anything to do with hurling because when he came, my hurling days were nearly over.'

Through the tennis club in Tallow, my father quickly got familiar with a number of people in the town. The young teacher also got involved with the drama society, an act that reflected his wide range of interests. The drama society was actually an offshoot of the tennis club and went under the official name of the Tallow Tennis Club Dramatic Group. A man from Youghal named Eddie Colbert was the usual drama coach and producer. Here again, Connie Ryan was a fellow traveller. I asked Connie if he remembered doing *Crime Comes to Ballyconneen* (see Chapter 4): 'It was a four-act play and it was one of the best plays we ever did… I was the "Boots" in a hotel – the man of all trades. I never saw that play since or read the book of it or anything but I made out that it had a plot second to none.'

His digs were upstairs in a corner building in the centre of Tallow, which was owned by a woman named Gertie Ronan. Here, he remained as a lodger for many years in typically loyal fashion. He was even joined by his brother Brendan at a later point when he too was working as a teacher in Tallow. At weekends, their diets were supplemented by his mother's home cooking.

While he was busying himself with using the few social outlets available to him during the working week, at weekends he was still a Dungarvan man. He would return home to his parents' house at the end of the working week and play football and hurling with the Dungarvan GAA club.

Eddie Bracken was a teacher who worked in Dungarvan from 1954 to 1956. While he was there, he also played with Dungarvan. But this coincided with a period of self-imposed exile from the club. My father had been spotted along with three other friends playing the banned sport of soccer in Quann's Field and was handed a six-month suspension. My dad was upset at what he saw was an excessive punishment but he was even more upset at the lack of assistance from the Dungarvan club in getting his severe treatment overturned. So when he went back playing football, he signed up with the rival Affane club.

He actually played with both Dungarvan and Affane during the 1950s. In or around 1953, he was spotted by a vigilant Waterford county board member committing the very serious sin of playing one of the 'foreign' team sports that was on the GAA's banned list. The 'ban' had been made as a riposte to the British ban on Gaelic games. It was, in fact, a counter-ban that was made in response to British authorities when the British were in power in Ireland and pursuing policies of cultural repression. This piece of knowledge actually makes the continuance of the ban all the more ludicrous in this day and age.

Even in Northern Ireland, there wasn't any ban by British security forces on their members playing GAA games. In fact, the opposite was true – it is the GAA's ban on members of the British security forces playing their games that has actually prevented the joy of GAA from spreading to armed employees of the Crown. This was surely a bit of a missed opportunity. I mean, had the British soldiers in the North been allowed to play GAA, then they might have developed a love of the games, which they would have taken home with them and spread throughout the dales and hills of rural England – very much in the same manner that the French troops learned to love rugby from playing it with their British allies in the trenches of the First World War. They then went on to play the game better than those who invented it. Come to think of it, maybe that was the fear: that the English would one day learn to play the game better than the native Irish.

In actual fact, Dad had not been lining out for any team whatsoever, but simply having a kick around in the famous Quann's field in Dungarvan with three other friends. But the ban was a weapon that was used with unforgiving ruthlessness when it suited and he was suspended by the county board (along with the three other transgressors on that day) for a period of six months. He had been playing for Dungarvan before the suspension and he was very dissatisfied at the lack of assistance he got from the Dungarvan board in getting the decision reversed or the punishment reduced. So, when he returned to the GAA field, he played instead for rival club Affane, with whom he had a connection in his aunt, before going back to play with Dungarvan at a later point.

Typically, he didn't make much of a song and dance about this. Eddie Bracken, even though he got to know my father well and they spent many hours in Quann's kicking ball in the company of others that included Tom Cunningham and Gary Morrissey, wasn't aware of the 'ban' story but felt that Dad was somewhat disenchanted with the GAA at the time.

'Your father used to play a lot of tennis at the time and was extremely fit and agile… He seemed to be a bit disillusioned with the set-up at the GAA. I wouldn't go as far as to say he was anti-GAA – my impression of him was that he wasn't the type of fella to get sour or bitter – but he was like a fella that had lost interest to some extent.'

But he kept playing hurling and football and he was knocking on the door of the position of county goalkeeper as a maturing player in his mid-twenties.

He also kept up with his social life in Tallow. In 1956, a young lady named Gretta O'Flynn from over the county border in Castlelyons arrived in town. She came fresh out of Carysfort teacher training college and into her first and only teaching post in the girls' national school in Tallow.

While the male teachers were all trained at St Pat's in Drumcondra, the female Catholic teachers of the nation were trained across town at Our Lady of Mercy College, Carysfort in the chic Dublin suburb of Blackrock. The college today is the Michael Smurfit School of Economics, part of UCD. The regime at Carysfort in my mother's time was far removed from liberal economics schools named after millionaires. It was similar to that of its fraternal college in Drumcondra, with the added 'uniform' of a black dress. My mother had come from a strictly run boarding school in Cahir, County Tipperary, however, so Carysfort to her was a breath of fresh air in comparison.

My mother has always told us how she didn't show too much interest in my dad at the beginning. It was through a mutual acquaintance by the name of Brian O'Sullivan that they were finally introduced to one another. Brian, a forester from West Cork, was a jovial uncle-figure to me growing up. He and his wife Nell lived in West End in Tallow: 'I was teaching their eldest daughter Anne and I used to deliver religious magazines. I was out once or twice to their house when Nell asked me in for a cup of tea and I got to know the two of them.'

One fateful evening, under the pretext of organising a debate at his house, Brian conspired to have my mother meet the athletic young teacher Ned Power (who was known to some as 'Eddie Power' at the time). Brian was fond of Mam and clearly considered Dad as highly eligible material for her and wanted to get her interested in Ned and away from the gentleman she was stepping out with at the time.

The strategy of Brian (or 'Blum', as he would affectionately become known to us) paid dividends in the end, of course, but it was not without its speed bumps. After the first night or two that Ned walked Gretta home (her digs were at the other end of Tallow – at Mrs Cox's on Barrack Street), she became interested enough to want to go out with him.

'He walked me down and said something like: "Would you like to come to the pictures some night?" I had this thing in my head that my mother used to always say to us – don't run after fellas: let them run after you – so I just said something like: "Well… I'll see." Then he said quickly: "Okay, sure as Brian O'Sullivan says, you should never rush a woman." He said goodnight and went off and I thought to myself: "Oh no… now look what you've done!" '

I always found that little story endearing – the frivolity of youth, the what-might-have-been element about it; how our very existence is dependent on the whims and the decisions of others far removed in time from us and yet, in hearing such stories, you have the comfort of knowing how it's going to end; that these two people are destined to get together. My own children, I notice, are equally fascinated by stories of how their mother and I first met.

Ned and Gretta were destined to be together. By the end of 1957, they were, to use the vernacular of the time, doing a steady line. At this point, my father was a Waterford senior inter-county hurler. He was substitute in the 1957 All-Ireland final – only one of six All-Ireland finals that the Waterford senior hurling team have ever contested – which they lost to Kilkenny.

My mother – a proud Cork woman – always likes to point out, however, that it wasn't until he was going with a Cork woman that he got a regular place on the Waterford team. She wasn't an avid follower of hurling, but with less other distractions to grab the attention of the plain people of Ireland, GAA matches occupied an even greater portion of the Irish psyche in those days than they do today. My mother would also have been aware of hurling rivalries from her time spent in boarding school in County Tipperary, as Cork and Tipperary were the two main hurling teams in that period and the Cork girls at boarding school would engage in good-natured ribbing with the Tipp girls.

'We were always fighting, even though we weren't too sure what we were fighting about. We'd be shouting at them about Christy Ring, but we wouldn't have known many of them.'

In her own digs, my mother was a bit more exposed to the world of hurling as John Cox – the landlord – used to talk a lot about hurling and about the promising young hurler Ned Power.

The cinema was the main social outlet in the evening in Tallow in those days. In the summer, there were also the Macra na Feirme outings. Both Ned and Gretta were members of the rural community network organisation – my dad was chairman and my mother was secretary of the Tallow branch. The Macra 'field days' were a great social gathering during the summer months. In common with most people, they still had no car before they were married, but they always managed to get lifts from somewhere, such as from Mam's friend and work colleague Eileen Cotter. There were various competitions at these occasions and my mother was amused to have won a little cup once for stock-judging and weeds & grasses.

From a professional point of view, a series of events conspired to fast-track my father into the position of principal of Naomh Mhuire Boys NS. One disadvantage of a teaching career is that promotion can be very slow and very limited and many teachers can go through a full working life without becoming principal. But when Mr O'Leary – the principal of the school at the time my father arrived in Tallow – died suddenly, my father succeeded him so that by the end of the 1950s, my father was principal of the boys' primary school in Tallow.

CHAPTER 8

MY FATHER, THE GARDENER

At the back of our house in Tallow, we had a decent-sized piece of ground that was known as the 'garden'. If I was to guess, I'd say that it was about an eighth of an acre. It was big – a bit too big to go turning into lawn. There was a lawn to the front which extended around one side of the house and there was a small side lawn on the other side. The rest of the ground around the house consisted of a tarmac drive and concrete yard. A wall was built when I was still young by a family friend and multi-talented handyman and professional forester named Mick Mulcahy, and this wall demarcated the yard from the garden.

Apart from one strip at the side which was a hen run, the garden was a mostly unused piece of ground which gave access to fields behind and the adventure that lay beyond. From my memory, there was one little piece of the garden that was used for growing vegetables. That's all I remember growing there. My mother was interested in creating an attractive garden with shrubs, flowers and trees and my father's interest lay strictly in nurturing food into life out of the back garden.

He was a dab hand at it because of his childhood experience tending vegetables in the little back garden of the family home in Dungarvan – when his own father had been billeted in Cork during the Emergency.

The garden produced a good range of produce. I remember as a child spending some time harvesting our potato crop and being amazed at how my father would dig out the potatoes carefully, shaking loose the soil. I suppose that, like all small children, I was easily enough impressed. Potatoes that had turned green from exposure to the sun were deemed 'sunny' by my dad and they were put aside for use as something other than consumption. The good potatoes were put into a wheelbarrow and the cargo was wheeled down from the garden to the yard, where it was transferred into bags. These were kept in the garage. This garage came complete with a door that opened with an up-and-over motion, but like most garages in Ireland, everything but a car was put into it. In fact, I remember it dawning on me one day at the age of 10 or 11 that this 'garage' really was an actual garage that had been designed specifically for keeping a car in it – just like in the American programmes on television. I was so excited by the discovery that I ran indoors to my parents to tell them the good news and to suggest to them that we put the car into it some time, maybe even straight away if they weren't too busy. They didn't.

In contrast to the gardening, at which my father was pretty good, indoor work was not his forte at all. He could do things that were useful outdoors but if he attempted to tackle any of the sort of interior handyman jobs that are commonly known under the banner DIY (even those in the garage), the results were awful, and sometimes presented a danger to others. There was one incident when my dad was commissioned by my mother to put up a shelf for the radio. In 1961, a radio set was a very large and heavy thing. My dad knocked a few nails into the plaster of the wall. These nails fastened brackets which held up a shelf, onto which was placed the very large and heavy radio set. When the entire thing fell one day amidst much noise and white dust into the cot where my sister Patricia would ordinarily have been found sleeping, my father made a conscious decision never again to attempt a DIY job. I'm pretty sure that he kept to this promise.

Maybe it was because I was smaller, but I do remember a time when the garden and the amount of produce it produced was much larger. I have a very clear memory from when I was probably three or four years old of walking through pea stalks that towered over my head, picking them off and eating them fresh and sweet from the pod. I don't think any vegetable has ever tasted so sweet again and we never did have peas since. I did wonder why afterwards because as far as I was concerned, they were the best thing that ever came out of the garden and one of the few products that I had no difficulty eating. But, from talking to other family members, it seems that the reason the peas never lasted was precisely because they were so popular. So popular were they that the peas were inclined to get eaten off the pod before they ever made it to the dinner table. So, those happy innocent childhood memories that I have of eating peas off the pod were probably of me as the smallest member of a family pea-raiding party, surreptitiously savouring sweet sweet peas while Dad wasn't looking.

The other pests that my father had to contend with were of the winged variety. Although he generally lived in harmony with most members of the animal and human world, he seemed to hold a special hatred for crows. 'Those bastards… BASTARDS of crows!' he would cry, running out and clapping his hands to clear them from the garden. I think that it was a mixture of total disrespect, persistence and bare-faced cheek that drove my father a bit crazy when it came to the crows, who, as far as he was concerned, had no place in a productive garden.

The other star performer from the garden as far as I'm concerned was the beetroot. My parents, and my dad in particular, were always encouraging us to eat food from the garden and I remember being introduced to a beetroot one summer. I developed a rapid fondness for eating it with salad cream – cutting it into juicy slices first. My father was delighted at my enthusiasm for his garden produce.

Some time around the era of my mid-teens, when half the family was gone out of the house, I remember that the garden had fallen into a much-reduced state of productivity. When my mother asked my dad about it, he answered something to the effect that the children had no interest in it. I felt a bit ashamed about that and it dawned on me that maybe I should have been more helpful with the garden, spreading the home-made compost and harvesting the food. But it's also true that part of my father's character was that he was a perfectionist and he tended to want to do everything himself and not delegate as well as he could have. In other households, some fathers might not have been quite as thorough as my father, but they knew how to delegate so that the jobs were always seen to.

CHAPTER 9

A GAA THOROUGHBRED?

There was no real tradition of sportsmanship in the Power family. In his own words, he says that his parents 'viewed hurling with tolerance and sympathy and no little affection'. In that sense, Ned was the first. His wasn't a family of sons following in their father's footsteps and brothers following their older brothers onto the field. Even my uncle Brendan – who, as the youngest brother in the family, tended to idolise my father and follow in his footsteps – did not take after his older brother in the realm of sports.

My dad was constantly kicking or striking a ball from a very early age. My uncle Seán remembers his brother repeatedly kicking a ball against the door with alternating feet, being missing down at Quann's for hours on end playing ball with Patsy Burke or listening intently and with religious regularity to the radio soccer commentary.

When he went to the CBS in Dungarvan for his secondary education, his love of GAA sports intensified and he got better as a player. He participated on the school teams in both hurling and Gaelic football. The school was strong in hurling at the time, as my father's former classmate Rory Wyley remembers: 'Even though our school wasn't the biggest, we were still able to take on all the other schools in Munster. It was a decent team.

'We were done out of a match against the North Mon,' he said, shaking his head at the memory of it. The North Mon is short for the North Monastery – a very prominent hurling school in Cork city and Dungarvan CBS had a shot at the Harty Cup title against them. This was the most important trophy for schools in Munster. The referee, he told me, was formerly a teacher at the North Mon and played eight minutes overtime in the final of the Harty Cup. North Mon got a late goal, giving them the lead and the final whistle was blown immediately after the ball went in the net. Johnny O'Connor – also playing on the team that day – confirmed this story, saying that the referee 'kept playing extra time and more extra time until The North Mon got the lead and then he blew the whistle. Oh, there was war over it!' His brother took off his jersey, threw down his hurley and walked away in disgust: Their one shot at the Harty Cup ended in a controversy that continues to inspire expressions of disgust today.

My father continued to play for his school and to play hurling and football for the Dungarvan senior team. Where did this love of sport come from? Maybe it's a question that doesn't really need to be asked. One of my dad's siblings that I asked that question of replied that in the poverty-stricken times of the 1940s and 1950s, there was 'nothing else to do'. There were certainly pubs, but my dad's people were not particularly pub people. In any case, it was a pastime that they, along with most others of the times, could ill afford.

I suppose that everyone loves sport to some extent. Sport is a microcosm of life, with its battles and entertainment, all within an organised and pre-arranged structure that mimics the structure of society itself. In my father's case, it just so happened that he began an interest in sport that grew with him as he got older. As a child in primary school, he got into the whole excitement of sports of all sorts. During his time in the Christian Brothers School, his talent for Gaelic games was encouraged and augmented and it was married with patriotism, which fairly increased its potency in the youthful Ned Power, coming as he did from a republican family.[1]

Ireland in the 1950s was a fairly depressed and repressed place. In comparison with today, there were few pastimes back then that met with the unqualified approval of the ever-present Catholic Church. Cinema, literature and other forms of entertainment were heavily censored.

Communion Kid
My father proudly displays his
Communion medal

Dungarvan Powers
The Power Clan, circa 1940. From left: Sean, Pat, Brendan, Dad, Kitty, Mary and Eileen

Dungarvan CBS Boys

A Dungarvan CBS team 1946 proudly displays the O'Callaghan Cup.
(My dad is third from right at the back)

Vibrancy of Youth
My father aged 19 in August 1949 at his Aunt Bridie's with two Continental lady friends.

Football Goalie
A rare shot of Dad in goals for Dungarvan playing with a larger ball in the early 50s.

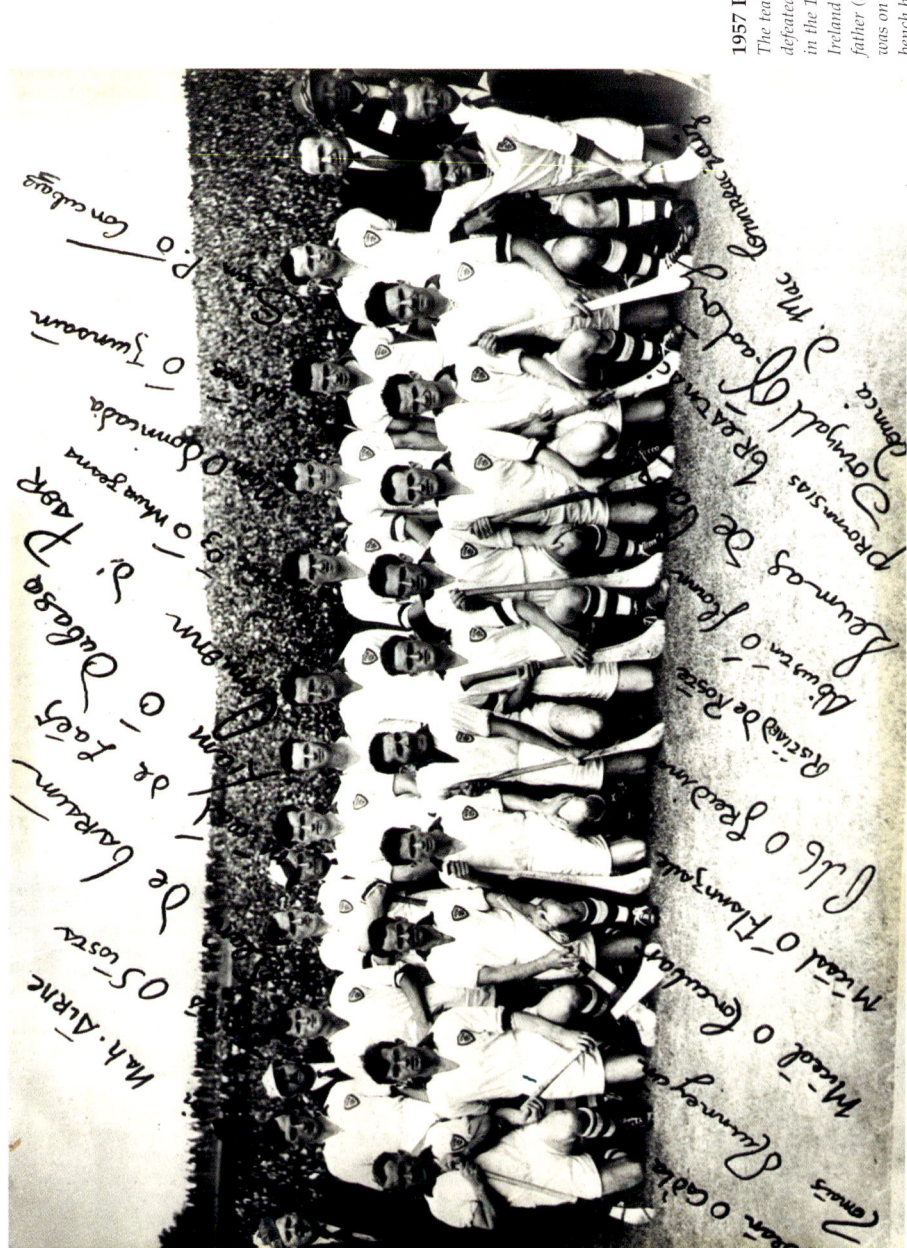

1957 Panel
The team that were defeated by Kilkenny in the 1957 All-Ireland Final. My father (centre, back) was on the substitute bench but didn't play.

The Little Touch

*A little touch from Dad is enough to see
off the threat of a Cork forward in the
Munster Final, July 1959.*

Congratulations!

*Waterford Mayor R. Jones keeps one eye on the camera whilst congratulating Dad
immediately after the 1959 Munster Final against Cork.*

Men of 1959

A picture taken just before their victorious All-Ireland final in 1959.
My father is at the back, third from left.

We've Won!
The eyes say it all. A shocked goalkeeper surrounded by well-wishers in the immediate aftermath of All-Irleland victory, 1959.

The Champ and his Best Girl
My mother congratulates my dad after the 1959 final in the shadow of the (then) new Hogan Stand.

Mean Streets
An armed officer of the law takes a name in his book. It was actually a cousin of Tom Cheasty (right) pretending to give him and my dad some hassle, New York 1960.

Wise Guys

Looking like a bunch of New Yorkers, Dad with (from L to R) Pat (Fox) Greaney, Tom Cheasty and Donal (Duck) Whelan.

Wedding Smiles

*Mam & Dad beam with delight on
their wedding day, August 11th, 1960.*

Banned authors at the time included Graham Greene, Samuel Beckett, Frank O'Connor and Austin Clarke. Activities that didn't fit into the ideal of the type of society that the Church had in mind for the young Republic didn't have much chance of flourishing.

But with GAA, the enjoyment was pure, uncensored and unbridled. It was the antidote to the depressing and increasingly economically desperate times. You had no job and you couldn't even afford your passage to England? Well, at least you could get yourself to the match on Sunday and cheer on John Keane for Waterford or Christy Ring for Cork and you could forget all your woes along with everyone else who attended the game.

What marked my father out from many other people involved in Gaelic games was his relentless pursuit of excellence. It is why he always excelled. It was his continual re-appraisal of himself as a player that made of him a good enough player to make the Waterford senior team and to get on that winning side. It was his pursuit of excellence that made him such a good coach. Because he was always looking to improve and learn and he was a perfectionist. And he pursued this perfection with a relentlessness that was persistence personified. Or, as my mother might say, stubbornness.

Séamus O'Brien – a Dungarvan man and former Waterford selector and long-time friend of my father's from his early days as a player – tried to sum up one of the defining qualities of Dad: 'As a senior hurling coach, he was very different to your ordinary run-of-the-mill fella. He was terribly meticulous, for example, about the condition of the pitch that he was going to play in. He always went to the trouble of making sure four or five days beforehand that the grass was cut to his satisfaction. It became a cant, in fact; "Would Ned Power be satisfied with that?"… I often remember him coming down to the field in Dungarvan a few days before an important match – maybe Tallow against Mount Sion in a senior county final – and checking the grass to see that it was cut to his satisfaction. If it was, he'd find the groundsman Paddy Fitzgerald and he'd thank him. And if it wasn't okay, he'd ask him something like; "What do you think about hurling? How can you expect the players to play on it when it's too high?" '

Whatever sport was available to him was good enough for the boundless energy and agility that he possessed as a youth. My dad was a dual player, representing his county and club in both hurling and football. For training, he kicked or hurled with friends at Quann's Field well into adulthood and he played tennis. The ban imposed on him for daring to play the foreign game of soccer in the early 1950s had dampened his enthusiasm for GAA games a little, but he persisted with it out of a love of sport that had been born within him and that was nurtured outside of his family environment.

How he ended up being a goalkeeper is something I'm not sure of because I never asked him the question. Even my mother wasn't exactly certain at how it all came about. Being the goalkeeper is a position that's a little different to everyone else and my wife – always someone who's good at asking the right questions – told me that Dad confided in her that he never really wanted to be the goalkeeper. No, he said: he wanted to play out the field, to be where all the action was. In the schoolyard, the goalkeeper is often the last person picked on the team. When it came to hurling, my dad always maintained that the opposite applied – you picked the best hurler to play in goal because the goalkeeper was the one who needed to have the best range of skills.

In any case, a goalkeeper is what he became. From 1954 to 1956, my father played in goals for the Waterford senior football team. After that, he began to tentatively break into the hurling team and when Waterford made it to an All-Ireland final in 1957, Ned Power was the named substitute goalkeeper. In 1958, at the fairly mature age of 28 and in the year that Pope Pius XII died, he made his debut as a first-choice championship senior hurler for Waterford. It was not to be a victorious start: Waterford suffered a 16-point defeat at the hands of Tipperary, who were on their way towards an All-Ireland title. The defeat, by all accounts, might have been heavier, were it not for the 'fine goalkeeping' by my father. And, as is the nature of annual championships, there's always next year…

CHAPTER 10

MY FATHER, THE MIMIC & ENTERTAINER

A couple of years ago, I was relating some story to a colleague of mine. I can't remember what it was exactly but it was something amusing that had happened in the office or out on the job. My occupation was as an auctioneer at the time and selling houses in West Cork for a living invariably throws up a regular supply of amusing anecdotes and incidents involving colourful characters.

In any case, as I was telling the story, my colleague smiled and interrupted me by asking: 'Can you not tell a story about someone without imitating the voice of the person in the story?'

My initial thought was 'No, I don't think I can.' As well as thinking it, I actually said it out loud to her, because I also thought that was funny. But afterwards, I did think about it a lot. Although she was amused by the whole thing, I began to wonder was there something wrong or weird about this habit that I had of always embellishing a story not with exaggeration as some people tend to do, but with trying to imitate to the best of my ability the voices of the characters involved in the story.

I decided that it wasn't weird – it was just entertaining – but the jury in my head was still out on whether or not it was wrong. I also realised that I did all of this almost subconsciously. I wasn't fully aware that I was doing it until it was pointed out to me by someone else. To me, it felt the most natural thing in the world to add in the voices when telling a story because my father did it all the time.

'Your father was always full of stories, no matter where he'd been,' my uncle Brendan told me in the context of talking about him as a child. 'And of course, he had the mimicry with it to give you an exact picture.'

So there you are – like father, like son. I notice that all of my siblings do it too to some extent; indeed, I'm not sure if any of them can actually get through a story about someone without imitating their voice.

My father was a very good mimic. He loved accents of every sort – the more peculiar, the better. His own accent could be described as a fairly neutral Irish accent and when he wanted to emphasise something in particular, be it in class or on the field or making a point about something or other at home, he would often throw in a strong accent from Kerry, Galway, Belfast or some other point of extremity. When he talked about New York and any incident connected with his visit there, he would affect a Manhattan drawl, complete with out-the-side-of-the-mouth delivery and hand gesticulations.

I think that it was the showman in him coming out. He would study comedians and entertainers in general and see how they would maintain an audience's interest as they went through their routine – warming them up and keeping them warm. Some of his favourites of the era were Tommy Cooper (for his apparent insanity and unique delivery), everyone at Hall's Pictorial Weekly (for the wicked satire) and Benny Hill (for his bare-faced good old-fashioned British bawdiness). I think he used to apply these sort of principles in many areas of his life: In the classroom where he had a testing young audience; on the hurling field; at home in front of his family; in front of his many friends and acquaintances. Basically, he was a man who was on stage a lot.

When he was good, he was good. Maybe everyone thinks their father is the funniest man in the world, but my father really was one of the most entertaining people ever. Even as a child, I was aware of the fact that each of us reckoned that our own dads were the tops when it came to entertainment, but it was when I saw the effect that his comedy act had on other children that I knew he was above the ranks of the ordinary father in this sense at least. Friends or cousins would regularly say to me: 'You know, your dad's awful funny!' usually just after my father would have got them giggling through one of his regular routines that I would have seen a thousand times before. I almost felt like saying: 'Yes, yes… It isn't bad – but you should hear his new material!'

I can remember him relating stories at the tea-time table about some character or other and getting me into such a state of hilarity that I couldn't eat. My sides were aching, my whole body would be convulsed in laughter and I would be blinded by tears in my eyes, with one hand propping up my head on the table. If there was any danger of my laughing subsiding, he'd say just one word to up the intensity again. I remember my mother pleading with my father through laughing of her own to stop and let me breathe.

Maybe we were all practice audiences for the real stage. The time he got to shine was when he was master of ceremonies for the Tallow Horse Fair Festival. This festival was the highlight of Tallow life when we were young. It went on for a week, culminating in Horse Fair Day at the beginning of September, when the whole place was taken over by horses, horse-dung and hawkers stalls offering all kinds of wonderful and exotic things, such as pump-action pop guns, water pistols or spud guns.

But every night, there was fun for all to be had on the open-air stage on the square. My dad would present event after event from early evening. There were singing contests, crisp-eating contests, a fancy-dress parade, balloon-blowing contests... whatever filled the time until the main act of the night came on, usually around nine o'clock, by which time I might have to be home again.

Occasions spent with my peers watching my dad on stage were amongst the proudest moments I've known. Although it's not something I've ever felt too funny about and certainly not ashamed of it, it's still not the coolest thing in the world to have a father who is the local school headmaster – not in front of your pals anyway. But when he was on stage on Horse Fair nights in the balmy evenings of the last week of the summer holidays, my dad was brilliant. I loved watching him keeping the show going with his professional presentation, piling on the quips and the laughs with an impeccable sense of timing, watching guys of my age laughing and turning around to one another, repeating a line that they had found particularly funny.

Then, when he was older and running the family home as a B&B with my mother, his MC character was brought to the fore once more. By then, he was retired from teaching and I think one of the aspects he missed most was the performance aspect of it in front of a regular audience. He kept the B&B guests amused in any case, with his endless repertoire of stories and conversation, which he would always steer around to hurling.

CHAPTER 11

1959 – THE PATH TO VICTORY

All-Ireland success came late in life for my father. He was just over a month and half from his 30th birthday when he finally got an All-Ireland winner's medal. At the time of writing, 7 out of the starting 15 of the Waterford team were still alive. Tracking down former team-mates of my father's is, I found, an intensely pleasurable and painful task.

It's a journey of discovery, feeling like so many film scenarios – where the detective or the son who never knew his father makes the journey after following the directions given to him by the man at the other end of the phone. The protagonist's face is tense and wide-eyed in anticipation as he slows down his car to cruising speed. He drives past lawn after lawn, checking each gatepost against the house number he has noted on a piece of paper which lies in the passenger seat of the car. All the mailboxes have their little flags standing to attention. It's a hot Californian day – quiet, with the occasional plump middle-aged man standing in his vest and holding a flaccid hosepipe, watering his lawn with a cigarette hanging loosely from his lips.

That was the scene of my call to the first man on my hit-list, except it was Dungarvan on a bright and breezy June day and where most cars go as fast as they possibly can. I was full of excitement, expecting only a jolly journey ahead, punctuated by laughs and smiles and maybe the occasional revelation. I had taken Austin Flynn's directions over the phone and memorised them – after the first roundabout, I was looking for a large, low building on the right. The large, low building didn't seem to present itself. So, I tried another road emanating from the roundabout. After a few kilometres, it quickly emerged that I was on the wrong road entirely, so back down the wide smooth County Waterford road I went to find the original road. By this stage, I was late by almost half an hour. I didn't want to be ringing him again for a number of reasons. Firstly, because I would sound a bit silly; secondly, because it would feel wrong to speak with him again and ruin the tantalising build-up to our meeting face to face; thirdly, because it felt appropriately old-fashioned to just get myself there as soon as I could without resorting to the over-use of such an acutely modern crutch as the mobile phone. I felt that someone of Austin's generation would appreciate such an approach. Besides, he had indicated to me on the phone that I needn't rush and that he would be in all afternoon.

I picked out a house on the right that, while not as substantial a building as the picture created in my head by Mr Flynn's telephone directions, was still a largish, lowish sort of house. More importantly, it had someone in the garden who might help me out. An electric hedge-strimmer lay silently on the ground amongst a confetti of clippings next to a freshly trimmed privet hedge. A man in a white shirt emerged. I removed my sunglasses like a Californian television detective, excused myself for the sudden intrusion and told him that I was looking for Austin Flynn's house. 'Straight across the road,' he said, with a speed of response so snappy I felt that he must have been pre-warned to expect a stranger looking for Austin Flynn. 'That's the man right there,' he added, pointing across the road. I turned to see my target standing in his lawn expectantly, in front of a large, low dwelling with a car-parking area to the side. So it was on the left, not the right. He had probably been watching me all the time.

Austin usually played full-back for the Waterford senior team during the same era as my dad, who considered him as possibly the best full-back ever. His greeting was friendly and he quickly scurried ahead of me ushering me inside. While I'm reluctant to use the phrase 'as giddy as a schoolboy', he did seem to be bent double in anticipation as he quickly gathered together his collection of photos and other paper data on my father.

This is where the seriousness and sadness of my task began to reveal itself to me. Your dad did this, your dad did that. I can see some of your father in your face. This is the picture of him as a young boy. Look… see? This is him here in New York, in Croke Park, with that shirt on, on that hot day. This is him in that famous photo. Here's me. You can't see my face. These are his classmates. This is it. This is all you have left of him – a collection of photos and pieces of paper, a man sitting across a table from you, imparting stories about what a great man he was, what a team-mate, what a perfectionist. Your father's dead and he won't be back, I'm afraid. We're here together speaking in a conversation being recorded by a digital recorder over a pile of circumstantial evidence precisely because your father is not here.

The reality of it all was like a loader full of bricks falling on me and around me as I tried to keep my speech and demeanour light and chatty. Although I had been pre-warned by my mother that it would be difficult to get away from the Flynn household on account of Austin's generous hospitality, I was released on time. Perhaps he sensed it – that I needed releasing.

*   *   *

I arrived at Pat Fanning's home on a typically cold and wet Irish summer's day. I had tried to use the satellite navigation system to find his house but his terrace didn't show up on it. So I had to use the old-fashioned method of following directions. Deprived as I was of the pleasure of using the 'sat-nav', Pat's directions were clear and I had no problem locating the tiny terrace behind the grotto. I could see why the mapping people had overlooked the terrace: it was a very short one defined only by a small change of angle in the street. The numbering system wasn't clear to me either, so I knocked on the door at one end. I had been told that Pat – who was at this time approaching the age of 90 – spent much of his time in a wheelchair. This house looked like it had an adequately altered front yard which was suitable for manoeuvring wheelchairs in and out. I rang the doorbell. After some time, a middle-aged lady appeared at the door in her nightgown. Although I had apologised for disturbing her, she dismissed me brusquely with a wave of the hand down the street, saying that he's 'down there' and then disappearing inside again before I could ask her to clarify. I knocked on the next door which I thought should logically be Number 3. A man emerged on his two feet. 'You're… Conor Power, from Tallow?' Right on both counts. He introduced himself as Jimmy Brown from Dungarvan originally and he had been asked by his neighbour Pat Fanning to keep an eye out for me.

I followed him down the street as he animatedly asked after my health and the well-being of everyone. He had recognised the 'foreign' Cork registration on my car.

Pat Fanning was the chairman of the Waterford GAA county board during the period. When I first met him in his house, he immediately apologised in advance for his lack of memory. In fact, he told me that Austin Flynn was the man to talk to. I told him that Austin Flynn had actually advised me to talk to him and had said that he was the one with the great memory. Pat had a good laugh at that. I asked him about his role in the 1959 team and suggested that he was the coach long before there was such a thing as an official coach.

'I suppose that's fair to say. John Keane was the team trainer… I was the one who did all the talking. I would talk to them before the game, during the game and after the game. I would do the motivating factor during that whole period. Your dad was one of the easiest to deal with – always co-operative, always at the very heart of the matter… They were a great bunch of boys.'

The 'boys' on the team travelled separately for training, with the Waterford city lads (who made up the majority of the team) travelling together and the lads from the west of the county going in another car. Normally, this particular car was driven by Mick Curley. Mick was a real live connection with a previous All-Ireland Waterford team, having played in the 1938 minor All-Ireland final and as a substitute on the 1948 All-Ireland winning team. The journey started with Ned in Tallow, before going on to pick up Tom Cheasty in Ballyduff and Austin Flynn in Dungarvan.

'Your father had a wonderful way with people,' Pat continued, giving me an example of one member of the team whom some players regarded as 'difficult'. 'Your father,' he said, 'had a great influence on him. [He] was always using humour to help diffuse any tense situations that could have ended up getting more awkward.'

Austin Flynn echoed this sentiment when he spoke about the healing influence that my dad seemed to have when there was any potential for difficulty or for a rift between personalities.

He also spoke of the bonding of the players in that Waterford team – how they got on with each other and gelled very well. Mount Sion man John Keane was the trainer of the team. He played in the only other

Waterford team to win a senior All-Ireland hurling title in 1948 and his influence as trainer of the team that was to win the 1959 senior All-Ireland title was a vital one, according to Austin Flynn: 'He was accepted as being the greatest hurler that Waterford had ever produced, but he was a lovely guy and he had a lovely approach.' The captain of the 1959 Waterford team Frankie Power described him to me as someone who would take you aside to talk to you about something you did wrong and would never dress a player down in front of his team-mates.

It must be kept in mind that there was a certain residual feeling of inferiority amongst some of the players from the smaller towns and villages of West Waterford when meeting people from the prestigious clubs of Waterford city such as Mount Sion. But, as Austin Flynn said, 'The Mount Sion lads went out of their way to make people like Ned Power and myself feel welcome.'

Another interesting point that emerged from talking to some of the players on the 1959 team is the relative lack of ambition that they had. There's no doubt that they wanted to win, that they had the will to do it and some of the lads on the team denied any suggestion of lack of ambition. But there seems to have been an altogether different kind of pressure on the players back then compared to that which exists today. Nowadays, GAA players at senior level are expected to be models of physical perfection. The county coaches are expected to deliver All-Ireland glory within a small number of years or they're unceremoniously booted out amid a cacophony of analyses, accompanied by anxious predictions as to the newcomer's chances of success.

Back in the 1950s, the game was a truly amateur one. There was no talk of compensation for time given or distance travelled. Players were expected to turn up with their own equipment – even for big games such as an All-Ireland final. For the replayed final of 1959, my father received the standard note notifying him of the date, reminding him of the importance of the game and detailing the pick-up and accommodation arrangements. It also requests that 'All players to have complete set of clean playing togs and hurley.'

Even though they're not mentioned in the brief, socks were to be provided by the players themselves. This non-provision of the most basic piece of a player's kit was the source of some griping amongst a number of players and my father went as far as underlining this situation by wearing mis-matching socks on All-Ireland day – neither of which were Waterford county colour socks.

'Your father had distinctive socks.' said team-mate and corner back Tom Cunningham. 'They were red and black. It didn't occur to me at the time, but I remember I asked him about it years later when I noticed it in a colour photo. This had gone past me altogether. In those days, the jersey was supplied, but you had supply everything else yourself… boots, shorts, hurley. According to your father, prior to the 1959 All-Ireland, there was some suggestion that the county board were going to supply stockings to the players. This was being mooted as a kind of gesture by the county board, but apparently this idea was not carried through and so everyone had to bring their own socks. So your father, as a protest against what he called a meanness on the part of the county board, decided that he'd go out and buy a pair of distinctive socks.'

Tom went on to say that my father didn't make much of a song and dance about his protest and it certainly wasn't picked up by any of the newspapers, whose analysis in those days made for shallow if somewhat more cheerful reading compared to today's publications. He just went about it in his own quiet way. There was some suggestion that Austin Flynn joined him in the Silent Sock Rebellion, but he denied it when I put it to him. For the Mount Sion lads, it didn't come into it as their blue-and-white club socks were the same colour as the county socks.

Coming up to the All-Ireland success of 1959, the dominant team was Tipperary. Having started the decade by completing a three-in-a-row in 1951, they re-established their supremacy on the hurling scene in 1958. That year, Waterford met them in the Munster championship. Instead of opting for a neutral ground in either Limerick or Cork, Waterford made the unusual decision of picking Tipperary's own ground in Thurles, the reason being that the wide pitch and the perfect sod would suit Waterford's expansive skilful style. As it turned out, Tipperary gave Waterford a solid beating, before going on to win the All-Ireland.

Between that year and 1967, Tipperary appeared in no fewer than seven All-Ireland finals, winning six of them. In 1959, they faced Waterford in the senior Munster semi-final. They were the stars on the rise, having beaten all-comers the previous year, sealing their All-Ireland victory with a convincing 10-point victory over Galway. They weren't expected to be bothered by Waterford. The Decies team was reckoned to be a good one all right, but not good enough to trouble the quality Tipperary team with a rock-solid defence.

As if the result could be in doubt, Tipperary had only three months previously despatched Waterford with relative ease in the final of the National League with an eight-point victory in a match which the

Evening Press described as a game of 'full-blooded hurling, frequently marked by over robust tackling'.

The Tipperary attack, with players such as Jimmy Doyle and Donie Nealon, was a force to be reckoned with but it was their beefy defence who were the superstars on the hurling scene at the time and its solidity had earned it the nickname 'Hell's Kitchen'. Well-known RTE GAA correspondent the late Mick Dunne was writing for the (now-defunct) *Irish Press* at the time. On the 1959 National League final, he wrote of 'the inadequacy of [Waterford's] attack against an almost impregnable defence…

> Many a Tipperary victory has been built on the county's great defence in the past. But never before have their backs so splendidly shown the superiority which is rightly theirs in the world of hurling. And at no stage of yesterday's final was their mastery so apparent as in 20 vital minutes of the second half during which Waterford enjoyed quite a generous share of the play and surged forward on repeated attacks… For even the Tipperary supporters in the 21,000 crowd the game was a disappointment. Tipperary shot into the lead in the third minute and were never afterwards overtaken.

Joe Sherwood – renowned sports editor and columnist with the *Evening Press* at the time – went even further in his praise of Tipperary's hurling prowess:

> The Tipperary team I saw beating Waterford in the National Hurling League final yesterday at Nowlan Park is a far better one than any fielded in the course of the county's championship triumphs last year, including the All-Ireland final against Galway… I would say that the only serious threat to Tipp losing their All-Ireland laurels is likely to come from Kilkenny… But let's get back to yesterday's match. I see not the slightest sign, in fact just the reverse, of any decline in the powers and prowess of Tipperary's magnificent defence… Without doubt this is the finest half back combination in the land, and possibly the best for ten years or so, I'll put it in front of Wexford's All-Ireland winning side of 1955-56… I am not going to be too critical of the Waterford forwards. They were eternally running up against an almost

impassable barrier. They were hunted and harried like a trapped fox with the hounds going in for the kill. On the odd occasions they did manage to break through midfield, they were faced with another almost impenetrable barrier. This was composed of Mick Byrne, dashing vigorous and lithe in his clearance, the big commanding Michael Maher and Kevin Carey, plus goalkeeper Moloney.

And so, to the championship. Waterford were one of the best teams going forward at that time. Their first-round opponents in the Munster championship was, unusually, a team from Connacht. Galway is a county that stands alone in hurling excellence in Connacht and they spent a decade competing in the Munster championship in the hope that it would improve their level of hurling. This experiment didn't quite get the desired results and they became the regular whipping boys of the Munster championship during their unhappy decade there. Waterford came through with a 7-11 to 0-8 thrashing of Galway. That same weekend, Ingemar Johansson had knocked out Floyd Patterson in a famous world heavyweight boxing title fight and Mick Dunne drew parallels between the two otherwise unrelated sporting events in his match report on the Monday:

> This was no game. Not after those opening nine minutes in which the Waterford forwards found cavernous gaps in the Galway defence and rammed through them to such shattering effect that the shock of it all was something like what Patterson must have experienced when he had his title whipped from him on Friday night.

Their next opponents were to be Tipperary with their Hell's Kitchen of a defence and their seemingly unstoppable winning ways. If victory was to be achieved against the premier county, it would surely have to be a narrow and hard-fought one. On July 12th, the day of the semi-final, the *Sunday Press* weighed up the situation between a skilful high-scoring Waterford team and a reticent winning Tipperary team that (as he saw it) stuck to their guns with simple hurling:

It is a difficult matter to forecast a result of this important test. I think it doubtful, however, that Waterford can succeed in toppling the champions.

Unlike the previous year's championship game, this one was going to be played on neutral ground – in the Cork Athletic Grounds, to be precise. Waterford were getting into their stride in the competition after their free-scoring 'warm-up' against Galway. They were also out to prove a point and were in determined mood.

'As far as I remember, Tipperary won the toss,' says Austin Flynn. 'There was a gale of wind there that day and Tipperary decided to play against it.'

There was, of course, no live television coverage in those days. If you wanted to experience a match, you got on your bike or a bus or you got a lift from one of the few people who had a car and you made your way to the game to see it live for yourself. It wasn't unusual, for example, for someone from Dungarvan or Waterford to cycle to Thurles or Cork – a distance that no man, woman or child would even dream of attempting today by bicycle unless they were in training for an important cycling event or were insane, or both.

If the match was considered important enough by the only broadcaster in the country – namely RTÉ – then it might warrant using tax-payers' money by sending commentator extraordinaire Micheál Ó Hehir to the event and setting up a live radio broadcast.

In this particular case, the result of the match was expected to be pretty much a foregone conclusion. It was therefore decided by RTÉ not to send Micheál to the Athletic Grounds in Cork (later to be rebuilt and re-christened 'Páirc Uí Chaoimh' in 1973) but instead he was despatched up to what promised to be a far more competitive Connacht football semi-final in Galway.

'At that time, RTÉ only broadcast one game,' says Micheál Ó Muircheartaigh, himself a well-known broadcaster and the very natural successor to Micheál Ó Hehir. 'Just one game and maybe a bit of a second one. They took a decision that time that it would hardly be worth broadcasting Waterford and Tipp' and it was the semi-final of the Munster Championship. Now, can you imagine the semi-final of a Munster Championship being ignored?

'Micheál Ó Hehir was sent to Galway – it must have been Galway–Mayo or something like that – but it was arranged that somebody would give him the half-time score from the Cork Athletic Grounds. And when he saw the piece of paper before him (he often spoke about it since): Waterford 8-3, Tipperary 0-0. Now, Tipperary were the League champions and the All-Ireland champions and Waterford were nobody. So, he refused to say it on air. He thought that somebody was having a joke. He scribbled a note for somebody to ring the Gardaí in Blackrock – the park was very near the Garda barracks – in order to verify the score.'

But there was no joke. Incredible as it seemed, the famously 'impenetrable' defence of the All-Ireland champions had leaked eight goals and the game was only half over. Paul Downey was a 14-year-old boy at that game. He and his brother had got a lift from a family friend who took them all the way from Kilmacthomas in East Waterford to Cork to see the match. Positioned behind the Blackrock goal end, their view wasn't great: 'They rained ball after ball into the square and although we couldn't see the net billowing the roar of the crowd and the green flag being waved, eight times in that first half hour, told us all we needed to know.' Equally astonishing was the fact that their canny forwards had been held scoreless. So what happened? What was Waterford's master plan that had deposed the rightful heirs to the All-Ireland crown in such devastating fashion? Did they even have a plan?

'We didn't really, no.' At just 21 years of age and already a veteran of Waterford's All-Ireland final appearance of two years previously, fiery forward Larry Guinan was the youngest on the team. On the day I met him, he was still putting in a day's work at his tyre business in Waterford city. Still as jovial and lively as he looks in those faded newspaper photos, he shakes my hand and tells me that I look like my father. He explained to me how the previous year's disappointments and the earlier defeat to Tipperary in the League had steeled their resolve to prove themselves.

'We were really out to do them that day,' said Larry, 'and it all came together on the day…. I got three goals against the famous John Doyle – that was sweet! It was brilliant, and they're still talking about it. It was a great team; we were all great friends, great comrades.'

'Liam Devanney – a great centre-forward – was on me,' recalls Austin Flynn of the same game. 'The match wasn't long in, to my recollection, and we'd a goal went in. That was okay. Then, there was another goal went in. And another, and another. Devanney started scratching his head and looking at me. He was obviously thinking: "Jesus, this is a nightmare. Is this really happening?" So I was conscious of that and I was trying to keep a straight face, as if it was par for the course, like. But I was as surprised as he was. What happened really was that Waterford had a great open style of hurling and it just happened that everything that day clicked.'

There was no real shock or sense of jubilation at half time in the Waterford camp, despite the huge lead they had built up, because they were all aware of the fact that they had another half to play and this time Tipperary had a gale-force wind behind them. On the Tipperary side, there was a strong sense of embarrassment and despair. Donie Nealon was playing midfield for them that day:

'I remember going out at half time – at that time, you went into an old shed in the Athletic Grounds. We didn't know where to turn. We hardly knew if we wanted to go back onto the field or where we should go!' There was to be no way back for the Premier County that day and it finished 9-3 to 3-4.

The next day, the newspapers expressed the shockwaves felt around the country from the sensational result. 'The fantastic has happened in Munster hurling,' screamed the *Cork Examiner*:

> Waterford have done to the mighty Tipperary exactly what they did to Galway – only more so. Against Galway it was five goals in twenty minutes but yesterday it was a matter of eight goals after twenty-two, a situation that left the 27,236 spectators at the Cork Athletic Grounds mesmerised. It was the most dramatic turn of events for years that Waterford should keep Tipperary scoreless in the first half and then go on to defy the obvious comeback and win through to the final against Cork. The final score of 9-3 to 3-4 is one for the records.

The *Irish Times*, at that time, offered relatively little coverage of Gaelic games. They hadn't bothered sending a photographer down to Cork for the match in this case, but they too recognised the magnitude of the result: 'Champions trounced by Waterford' they announced in the headline of the match report, which reads rather like the information was attained second hand, but at least the anonymous writer had the good judgement to list a certain 'E Power in goal' first in its list of 'outstanding players'.

Next up was the Munster final and arch-rivals Cork. A county which never fields a weak team, this one was a strong one too and featured Cork's most famous hurler of all time – Christy Ring. The robust centre forward was supremely gifted and, along with the afore-mentioned John Doyle of Tipperary, holds the record for the highest number of All-Ireland medals won (eight). Even by the time my father and his team-mates stepped onto the field in Thurles on a sweltering 26th of July day in 1959, 'Ringy' was already a legend.

He was a legend that my dad came across regularly during this era in championship competition and they were as friendly with one another off the field as they were competitive on the field. In one of these games, Ring tried to score a goal on Dad but my father saved. All fired up in the heat of battle, he threw the ball mockingly at his opponent, shouting: 'Here, Christy… Have another go!' Some years later, Ring faced my dad again in a championship match. This time, the Cork forward scored. As my father prepared to pick the ball out of the net, Ring raced into the goal and snatched the ball. As he ran back to his position, he turned and threw the sliotar at my dad and shouted: 'There you go, Ned… Have another go!'

The stage was set for a fascinating duel, which drew a record attendance for a Munster final of 55,174 (with record gate receipts of IR£6,728). By now, Waterford had proven themselves as serious All-Ireland title contenders, having humiliated the reigning champions, and it was difficult to predict how the game was going to go, with Waterford remaining slight favourites.

As it turned out, the match was a cracker, winning praise from all quarters for its high level of skill and its intensity. The *Cork Examiner* described it as 'Rip-roaring Hurling', the *Irish Independent* as an 'Epic Final'. The late Philly Grimes of Waterford dominated the midfield and although Cork took a three-point lead after six minutes; it was Waterford who went in at the half-time break with a four-point advantage. In the second half, the Waterford dominance continued and, with nine minutes to go, they were leading Cork by eight points. Cork weren't finished yet, though, as John Hickey of the *Irish Independent* describes:

> Nine minutes from time, Waterford followers were quite composed, and with good reason, as their side then led by 3-9 to 1-7.

> But Cork who had hurled defiance at Waterford, when they elected to play against the slight wind and sun – I am convinced it was a pre-arranged stratagem – were by no means a spent force.

> Nine minutes from time, Christy Ring pointed from a 21 yards free; three minutes later Barry followed with a like score; and then $5^1/2$ minutes from the call of time, a

wonderful goal by Ring put the Munster trophy in the melting pot once again.

There followed a period of breath-taking escapes and near misses, particularly in the Waterford goal area, that simply beggared description.

I was so enraptured, captivated by the splendour of the fare, that I quite forgot to make a solitary note during that wondrous finish.

But one incident in it stands out in my mind as clearly as if I had been the 'culprit'. It was a near miss by Barry when Waterford goal-keeper Ned Power made a splendid save and then had to bring the ball right across the goal before getting in a clearance that prevented the losers levelling the score.

That was the major happening in an inspiring finish that will be discussed as long as those who saw it talk hurling and hurlers.

Now, as I relive those delightfully distressing minutes, my one regret is that the closing stages of the contest were not filmed – then we could see it again and again.

The match produced some great action shots, including ones of my father doing his bit in goal. Even the *Evening Press* of the following Tuesday 'just couldn't resist' showing the one of my dad catching the ball in his hand in mid-air, denying Barry's final goal effort which would have made the match a draw (the final score was 3-9, 2-9 to Waterford).

In his column on that Tuesday, Joe Sherwood gives some time to describing the chaos that the large crowd seems to have caused, resulting in journalists having difficulties in entering the stadium.

Not since I was a kid, had I broken into a football stadium until last Sunday. After paying two bob I think it was to pass through the outer gate admitting me to the Thurles GAA Stadium – this after vainly trying to reach the official entrance – I was no better off than if I had stayed outside. At an inner gate, leading I take it to the side line and attendant who I took to be the guardian of what I visualised the Bastille must have looked like, peered from behind a stout iron bar. I explained in a few brief words I was a reporter, and apparently the old pipe gave me away, because the guardian of the second bastion behind the iron bar told me whether in anger or in fun 'that I was the last man he would let in' because I had written something about Tipperary which had displeased him.

Now, for the second time in three years, Waterford were in an All-Ireland final. And, for the second time, their opponents were Kilkenny. Across the Irish Sea in England, film actor John Gregson wrote to the GAA Headquarters requesting a ticket for the final and permission to line out with the Waterford players. Two years before, Gregson had starred in *Rooney*, a film in which he played a Dublin dustman who turns to hurling. It was a minor hit and one of the few high-profile films to have featured hurling in its plot. For the scene in which his character lines out for the All-Ireland final, Gregson tagged along with the Kilkenny team. He had requested to join the Waterford team but the response was not in the affirmative so he ended up on the Kilkenny team for that opening shot. Even now, if you look carefully at the footage of the 1957 All-Ireland final, you can clearly recognise Gregson as the 16th man in the Kilkenny team as they perform the traditional march behind the Artane Boys Band. Whether or not Gregson got a ticket for the match, I don't know, but in any case he wasn't going to line out with the Waterford team this time either.

CHAPTER 12

MY FATHER, THE WRITER

In the *Dungarvan Leader* of Friday, November 23rd 2007, there was a long and heart-rending tribute to my father which I still find difficult to read. One of the paragraphs is devoted to talking about my father as a writer and it reads:

> This man of many talents could have made a living as a journalist had he chosen that path. As the French would say, he had une belle plume and his weekly articles on the local papers brought him a complete new constituency of devotees. He would be controversial and like some more of us ended up in water occasionally for his forthright views. His writing on a range of subjects from coaching to referees are worth preserving. There was a great book in the man.

I liked the way that it said he had a *belle plume*. I imagine that he would have smiled at that one, being described in somewhat magical and mysterious terms as a possessor of a writing instrument that produced beauty wherever it went. Certainly if you see his handwriting, it does look like it has been written using a *belle plume* – all flourishing perfection of the type that is a rarity in today's Ireland.

My father's regular writings in the *Dungarvan Leader* were cut out and kept by my mother and, as I write, I'm in possession of the large pile of yellowing pieces of newsprint. Being a perfectionist in everything he did, and reading through them now with the benefit of an editor's eye, I can see that they are all well-written and well-finished articles, written in a style that's clear, eloquent and easy to read. I also get a sense of discovering more about my father. There were a lot of things he was concerned about or annoyed about or amused about and I try to place myself at the time of writing of each article.

There's one on Waterford beating Cork from February 1996, for example. If that was today, I would be far more interested and I'd have read up the match report if I hadn't watched it live or on television. It made me wonder just what was going on in my life at that time when I had little if any interest in the fortunes of the Waterford senior hurling team. I was recently married and a father of small baby at the time, so I suppose that there wasn't much room for GAA in my life.

Those articles from the mid- to late 1990s often made some very salient points about GAA matters and my dad was not one to pull any punches when it came to talking about hurling or the GAA in general. For some first-class controversy, however, one needs to go a little further back to a time when his more direct involvement in the game seem to give his writings a sharper edge – an edge that sometimes drew blood.

In 1971, he wrote in the *Dungarvan Leader* about an incident with the Shamrocks GAA club and Tallow. Shamrocks is a club name that's found all over the country and it usually refers to a club consisting of three rural parishes playing under the one banner. In this case, the parishes are Knockanore, Kilwatermoy and Glendine. Its proximity to Tallow means that there was always a healthy degree of rivalry that would occasionally boil over if people weren't careful with their words.

In the middle of a match between Tallow and the Shamrocks that year, the news came through at half time that the Shamrocks team was eight points up. There was a 'Shamrocks' pub in Tallow at the time out West Street named Mulcahy's and was owned by the late Din Mulcahy. When the news came through at half time, a decision was made to prepare a large batch of chicken sandwiches to feed the jubilant and hungry Shamrocks supporters that would surely be arriving victorious after the match.

But victory was snatched from the Shamrocks that day. As the story filtered through about the superfluous quantity of uneaten chicken sandwiches and the premature decision of making them based on a half-time score, those in the Tallow camp found the scenario particularly hilarious. In his column in the *Dungarvan Leader* that week, my father simply could not resist referring to this sorry symbol of The Shamrocks' premature presumption of victory. 'The moral of the story is,' he said in a thinly veiled reference to the incident, 'don't count your chickens – cooked or uncooked – until they're hatched.'

Those in the Shamrocks camp did not see the funny side of it. There was a written, anonymous reply (widely believed to be from a certain James Tobin) in the paper the following week, to which my Dad replied again in his column. This continued for a number of weeks and it became a minor soap opera in its own right, greatly boosting sales of the *Dungarvan Leader* in the Tallow area.

There was another incident which threatened to go as far as court proceedings. A certain young under-12 hurler from Ballyduff was singled out by my father in his column in the *Dungarvan Leader*. Some unforgiving things were said with regard to his behaviour which my father described as 'loutish'. In addition, my dad also made reference to his coach, saying that whoever coached him ought to be ashamed of themselves. Naturally, neither the boy's parents nor his coach were happy with what he said. As ever, my father would not be for retracting things that he would have said or written in the first place because he saw them as the truth.

Speaking the truth as he saw it was something that was never up for negotiation. He was an affable and genial person who would never go looking for a fight. But if he felt that something was wrong and that that needed to be said clearly, then he would say it and damn the consequences. There was another incident with a *Dungarvan Leader* article in the early 1990s that I was certain of having happened. This is how I remember the sequence of events: Having witnessed an All-Ireland football championship match involving Meath, he wrote a piece in which he referred to the Meath players as 'Tramps' because of what he saw as their excessively brutish behaviour. He wouldn't change the article or remove the word 'tramps' from it. The article wasn't published and my father stopped writing for the newspaper.

I asked everyone in my family and I asked a number of friends and acquaintances who might have known. I couldn't believe that nobody else remembered it because I seem to remember talking to my brother

Éamonn and others about it. So, I contacted the editor of the *Dungarvan Leader* to see if he remembered anything about this. When I introduced myself to Colm Nagle over the phone, he was most helpful, saying that he would be delighted to assist in any way.

Colm could not remember much about the incident. He did recall that it was an inflammatory piece and that part of the reason it wasn't published was because the subject had already been covered by a national daily newspaper earlier in the week so its relevancy would have been lost. The other issue, of course, was that as a small provincial newspaper, one had to be careful about printing insulting or inflammatory remarks about people.

His GAA columns did resume after a few years and they continued to be read by a lot of people locally. I think that it is a pity that he didn't turn his writing hand to something else other than the sport he loved because there's no doubt in my mind that his command of the English language (or, indeed the Irish language) was such that he could have been a journalist or a novelist or a playwright. His strong command of English goes back to the relatively poor mark he got in English in his Leaving Certificate back in 1947. Since then, he strove to improve his vocabulary. The multiple hours he clocked up reading newspapers were used, amongst other things, to improve his vocabulary and he would systematically underline any words he didn't understand, which he would look up in a dictionary later. But, I suppose that his life revolved so much around GAA that he was always destined to write about one thing only.

CHAPTER 13

CHAMPIONS AT LAST!

The *Waterford News & Star*'s report on July 31st looked forward with some relish to the September All-Ireland final and reflected the confident mood in Waterford as well as the choice of opponents:

> Equally certain is the fact that, given the choice of opponents for this year's final, Waterford, to a man, would plump for Kilkenny. The disappointment of '57 is still fresh in the memory of Waterford, and now they have a golden opportunity of reversing the decision of that fateful year. Defeating Kilkenny in the final would add extra lustre to the big gold medal with the harp in the centre.

The front page carries a great photo of my dad – looking his most handsome, I think – shaking the hand of the Mayor of Waterford just after the Munster final against Cork. The mayor is looking very smooth in a fine suit and hat. My dad is obviously saying something to him; it looks like his thanking him for his kind wishes, but the mayor's eyes are wide and looking straight into the camera lens. I don't know what kind of person the mayor was, but in this shot he looks the epitome of the politician who has just found a great photo-opportunity.

Meanwhile, the Waterford team continued their preparations for the big final. Training in those days was a very different approach to the semi-professional style of preparation that teams engage in nowadays. Training at an official level consisted of preparing players physically for the match, but had nothing to do with honing their skills. For that, some of the players who were perfectionist in nature took it upon themselves to literally train themselves. Midfielder Philly Grimes was one of them and so was my father and the two would often engage in setting up end-of-match do-or-die scenarios, testing one another on their respective skills.

Training nights would normally take place in Waterford, or occasionally in the Fraher Field in Dungarvan. All members of the 1959 team speak of the special bonding that the team had. One important element of that bonding was that the men from the west of the county would usually travel together in a hackney car that was invariably driven by Mick Curley (who himself of course had been a goalkeeper on the Waterford panel on the 1948 All-Ireland winning team). Austin Flynn remembers how important a part those trips played in the bonding process:

'Part of that process – although it might seem strange now – was the hackney driver. Fellas didn't have cars at that time, so you had Mick Curley of Tallow bringing Ned and they'd be picking us up in Dungarvan going to training. So there was always a laugh and a joke and we felt very free with each other. Now, we thought that that was normal but it was years afterwards that somebody told me about other teams where people travelling in the same car weren't on the same wavelength at all…

'There were many days when we suffered terrible defeats too, but even in defeat we were able to laugh at ourselves. So there was a great bond and that carries on to this day. Your father was a great fella with people and he knew everybody. There wouldn't have been many social occasions that time because you generally played your match and you went your own way afterwards. But if there was a social occasion, I'd often tag along with Ned, who'd be talking to everyone. I'd be whispering to him "Who's your man?" and he'd be roaring laughing at me because I didn't know who they were.'

One of the team's strengths that was widely recognised at the time was its speed. The official team trainer John Keane would have the players playing 'chase the ball', flicking the ball along the ground just out of a player's reach so that he'd have to move fast to get it. He was also careful not to overdo the physical training – again something relatively experimental at the time. But John was an experienced All-Ireland medal winner who knew the importance of not overdoing physical exertion and of keeping one's skills sharp.

September 6th came. The day of the final. Most newspapers were predicting a Waterford victory. This was, after all, the team that had so mercilessly despatched the Tipperary team and had overcome Cork. In the *Sunday Review* that day, the prediction from its hurling correspondent and former Waterford trainer Paul Russell was that the 'Powerful Decies Selection Should Take the Cup'. He had attended a training session of the team and wrote of his impressions which echo those of Austin Flynn and other members of the team:

> I found them the most relaxed, joyful bunch of lads you could find in any training camp. They were unworried… unruffled… and in the peak of condition. Their sprinting, walking, jogging, trotting, and hurling was a joy to watch – training methods that only the perfect athlete could perform. I pointed all this out to John Keane and he said: 'Yes, Paul, they are a fine bunch of lads. Believe me, this is our year. We know the Kilkenny lads; we are not underestimating them, but we will play for the full hour – and win.'

'I agree with him,' adds Pat Fanning in the same report. 'Never have I heard a hurling final discussed so much by the players, mentors and trainer. They are just eating, drinking, sleeping this hurling final today.'

In the *Sunday Press* that day, Éamonn Mongey presciently asks if the match, like the two sides' first meeting 73 years previously, will end in a draw. In what was the first 'final' day for what was then the new Hogan Stand, the game did end in a draw. Although Waterford (1-17) scored almost twice as many times as Kilkenny (5-5) did, this time it was Kilkenny who got the vital goals in a year where Waterford were the ones who clocked up a high goal tally. That fact must have been a disappointment and a worry for the Waterford team going into the replay, as well as the fact that the match was only saved by Waterford's only goal, which was scored in the dying minutes of the game by Séamus Power.

The last moments were so frenetic that there was confusion amongst many players on the team as to who was winning. The scoreboard didn't show the aggregate score – only the score in goals and points – so the players and spectators had to perform their own mathematics to work out who was winning.

That's not an easy task when you're also preoccupied with trying to play in an All-Ireland final. Captain Frankie Walsh went into the dressing room in a dejected mood, thinking that they had lost while his county and club team-mate Séamus Power was convinced that they were All-Ireland champions: 'Séamus thought we were a point ahead and I thought we were a point behind. Sure I was going off the field thinking we were beaten by a point again!'

The national dailies were fulsome in their praise of the match the following day. 'Thank heavens it was a draw,' wrote John D. Hickey in the *Irish Independent*. 'That was my predominant thought at the end of an epic combat at Croke Park yesterday, when, in an All-Ireland senior hurling final that simply beggars description, a game that seems to make all words inadequate, Waterford and Kilkenny ended on level terms in a contest that must rank as a landmark in the history of the GAA.'

In the *Cork Examiner*, an equally breathless report speaks of a 'Thrilling Climax to a Rousing Final'. In his 'In the Soup' column in the *Evening Press*, Joe Sherwood waxed lyrical about the drawn final:

> What a rousing grand stand finish there was in the All-Ireland hurling final at Croke Park yesterday…
>
> The opening half, even though Waterford had asserted their superiority to win a 0-9 to 1-1 interval lead, was waged at top speed with neither side sparing itself. But this was made to look like a jog trot compared with what was to come after the change of ends.
>
> Then for thirty minutes, fury was let loose. What heart-palpitating stuff it was. Never a moment's respite for either players or onlookers. It seemed unbelievable that humans could keep going at such a pace. The harder Kilkenny hit to win their way back into the game (which they succeeded in doing), the harder Waterford hit back.'

Sherwood surmises that the 'aerial game paid off' for Kilkenny in the second half:

One imagines that at half-time they must have had a parley among themselves, and then returned to the fray to play Waterford, not at their own game which was ground hurling, but to swing the ball through the air with mighty goal-mouth pucks. And they soon discovered Waterford's Achilles heel. So they played on it… They [Waterford defenders] must now know what to expect in the replay on October 4. Whether they have learned their lesson remains to be seen… Wasn't it a game to last in memory with the greatest ever played in Croke Park? How the boys lasted out the hour at such a pace is indeed a rare and lasting tribute to our young manhood.

Possibly one of the most impressed neutral observers at the game was one Kenneth Wolstenholme – a BBC commentator who had come over with a camera unit to make a brief documentary on the sport for a British sports programme. 'If you took those teams on a world tour to play a game like that you would have hurling played everywhere,' he enthused in the *Evening Herald* the day after the game. 'The amazing speed of the game simply thrilled me… I could not understand how they could control the ball with those pieces of wood. And the wholehearted body contact just had to be seen to be believed. I had expected to be interested in the match, but it was not long in progress before I was a real fan. Most games have their dull moments, but this hurling is "go" all the time!' He singled out Tom Cheasty as the star of the game and went to the dressing room afterwards, where John Keane presented him with a souvenir hurley.

Wolstenholme's prediction of world domination for the Irish national game is an interesting one when, half a century later, the game is shown live around the world. The *Herald*'s hurling correspondent echoed the hope of growth in popularity that the game elicited in his report: 'Hurling may not be making headway in many counties, but a few more epic hours like yesterday's All-Ireland final… could well make the caman [sic] game even more popular than Gaelic football.'

October 4th – almost a month later – was the date set for the replay. On the Thursday before, Mick Dunne wrote in the *Irish Press* of Waterford hopes still being high. Even though the mood of the fans was 'puzzled and a little worried', the players, he maintained, were 'pleased that the bubble of super-optimism which surrounded their first meeting with Kilkenny has been burst. Now they feel that the replay will be approached with a more reasonable attitude.'

Training sessions were kept light and two changes were made, with Mick Flannelly (who had previously played in the preceding year's Munster final) coming in at right half-forward and Tom Cunningham – who normally played in defence – taking the full-forward position.

'We had to change our tactics,' Frankie Walsh told me as we sat in his house in Waterford city. 'The backs needed a bit of toughening up so we did "backs and forwards" training.' In other words, it was decided that the team would engage in role-play and try to re-create situations where the forwards would be running onto the backs and the backs had to train themselves to defend better than they did in the drawn game.

As the day approached, expectations from the Waterford public went to fever pitch.

> On Sunday next, reported the Waterford News & Star two days beforehand, there will be a great gathering of Waterford folk to cheer the locals on to the greatest effort. Ten trains – including three direct from Waterford – will leave various centres with an estimated 12,000 fans, while thousands of others will get there by various other modes of conveyance. Included in the crowd will be members of the Waterford Association in London, who will come back to Erin and mingle with their own for the great day.

Even though the team had leaked five goals in the first game, the general analysis was that it was the failure of the backs to defend my father, rather than any failing on his part that was to blame. In any event, no changes were made in the defence and the *Déiseach* of the *Waterford News & Star* wrote:

> Give Ned Power the cover and he need not stand in the shadow of Ollie Walsh [the Kilkenny goalie who got much praise for his performance in first game] or anybody else. In fact, the Dungarvan man, on the basis of his performance between the Waterford posts, is in the top flight of net-minders.

Going into the replayed final, the average Waterford player was a year older and a pound heavier than his Kilkenny counterpart, but most analysts favoured Waterford not to repeat the mistakes of the first game and to claim victory.

Forward Larry Guinan was in confident mood during the four-week hiatus between the two finals: 'I felt we were good enough to win… we had a really good team and we'd been knocking on the door for a while and I felt that we should win something.'

In an interview that my dad gave for the TG4 television series *Laochra Gaeil*, he says that they were 'a lot more settled and a lot more focused on the task ahead' for the second match.

As the legend of the quality of the drawn game spread, Waterford and Kilkenny supporters and GAA fans from around the country were all keen to get to Croke Park. The attendance figure of 77,285 was very high (3,578 more than at the first game) and it was the first time since 1931 that the attendance figures in either code for a replay exceeded those of the drawn game. An estimated 8,000 people were turned away for fear of overcrowding. Even though it was into the second month of autumn and the clocks had gone back to winter time, the day was sunny with reported temperatures of up to 23?.

In my possession as I write is a match programme of the big day. It's a simple A5-sized paper document with the barest of information. Running to just eight pages in all, it gives the names (although not the clubs or the ages) of all the players involved in both the junior and the senior matches; an uncredited foreword; the role of honour to date; details of the officiating referees (E. Connery of Laois refereed the senior match); and just two advertisements – one for Clerys and one for Sweet Afton cigarettes. The 2008 match programme runs to 100 pages.

Also amongst my dad's memorabilia is his official letter from Waterford County GAA Board, at 17 Temple St., Dungarvan, requesting his presence at the All-Ireland final. It's a standard typed letter with blanks that are filled in with blue pen in a mixture of Irish and English:

A Chara, it begins. *Kindly note that you have been selected on the Waterford SH team to play Cill Coinnaigh at P. an Crócaigh on Sunday 4/10/59. You are requested to make yourself as fit as possible in preparation for this very important engagement. If, for any reason, you are not available to travel, you are requested to notify me in writing at the very earliest, so that a substitute may be selected to travel in your place.*

Players failing to notify me of inability to travel or field out will be reported to the County board.

Players will travel by car on ~~Sunday~~ [sic] Saturday 3/10/59 and you are requested to meet car at home 1.30 Tallow.

All players to have complete set of clean playing togs and hurley.

Teams will stay at the Grand Hotel Malahide where you are asked to report on arrival, not later than 6.30 S.T.

Mise,

The game started poorly enough from a Waterford perspective. Although they had the strong breeze behind them, it was Kilkenny who went into the lead, scoring a goal and a point without any reply. A goal from Mick Flannelly seemed to settle the Déise team and a Tom Cunningham goal minutes later saw them take a lead that they would not relinquish for the rest of the game. It finished 3-12 to 1-10.

None of the defensive errors that had almost cost them the first match were to come back to haunt them.

> Their defensive tactics paid off handsomely,' *noted Seán Óg Ó Ceallacháin in his match report in the Evening Press the next day.* Close marking and quick tackling stifled the best efforts of the Kilkenny forwards right through the game. Above all, and I thought it stuck out very noticeably, the Noreside forwards were not allowed to crowd the Waterford goalkeeper to the same extent as the drawn game.

Sure enough, looking through the footage of the two matches, you can see a lot of Dad getting clattered and picking himself up in the first game, but in the images of the second game, it's all shots of long puck-outs with space before him and head held high with his eyes firmly fixed on the victory that was already clearly visible.

> …goalkeeper Ned Power, this time given a fair chance to see what was coming at him, did his stuff cleanly, crisply and with confidence. And let me add, his goal pucks were of greater length than Ollie's.

The inimitable Joe Sherwood so described my dad's performance on the big day. And just to show that outbreaks of ill-discipline are nothing new, there was one incident of note that Mr Sherwood colourfully described where things turned violent:

[There was a] bit of a 'barney' in the Waterford goalmouth in which eight or more players indulged in a mixture of all-in wrestling and fisticuffs. Jim [sic] [Barron of Waterford] and Dick [Carroll of Kilkenny] restarted a little feud on their own in which some timely punches were exchanged in the clinches. And the referee just couldn't do anything else but 'retire them' to the sideline. But the culprit who started off the spark that led to the shindy got off scot-free. And he wasn't a Waterford player.

None of the surviving team wanted to go mentioning names at this point as to who started the fray, but Frankie Walsh did say that 'John Barron didn't deserve to get sent off – They all agreed on that.'

Ugly incident aside, the papers were unanimous in their praise of the match, of Waterford' performance and of the deserving nature of their win, as well as of the quality of the championship overall.

Hail Waterford, the new holders of the All-Ireland hurling title, *effused Mick Dunne in the* Irish Press. Champion among champions are these white and blue clad men of the Decies. For this second championship, which they won so splendidly in Croke Park yesterday and now take across the Suir for the second time, must surely stand apart as the greatest by far of the 72 championships that have now been played in the 75 years of the GAA.

With justifiable pride they can wear their All-Ireland crown. As no other team before them has done – they have won it in the hardest possible manner in an extended championship. For on the way to this triumph they have conquered Galway, Tipperary, Cork and now Kilkenny – counties that have between them taken 51 of the All-Ireland titles.

A half a century later, the championship is even further extended. As I write, the game is still an amateur one (from the point of view of the players, at least), as it was back then. Even with the extra game of a replay, the players never had less than four weeks preparation time for the next game during the championship campaign of 1959. The squeezing of the maximum matches into all the available time-slots that characterises the modern GAA championships means that amateur sportsmen are expected to be match-fit within a week, sometimes having to play three big deciders three weeks running.

Another point of note made by Mick Dunne in the same paper is his allusion to the fears of some that the Waterford hurlers would be 'burned out' by such a rigorous campaign of matches and training. If it was felt that players back then were in danger of being burned out by a schedule that looks like a walk in the park compared to that of today's GAA stars, what should we feel now?

My dad remembered that it was Kilkenny goalkeeper Ollie Walsh who was the first to come to congratulate him after the match. He was so warm and genuine with his felicitations, said my father, that the memory of it stayed with him for the rest of his life. I think the two goalkeepers had a lot of time for one another. Ollie once confided in my dad that his secret ambition was to save a shot during a big match, solo out with the ball and score a point at the other end – something which he did attempt against Waterford on a different day , although he never got beyond the half-way line. On the occasion of Ollie's death in 1996, my father wrote of him that he 'never met a jollier or a sunnier character, nor a more exciting or thrilling performer than my friend Ollie.'

In any case, it was a happy Frankie Walsh who, as team captain, was carried shoulder-high by the crowd and who mounted the famous steps to accept the Liam McCarthy Cup from GAA president Dr J.J. Stuart in the presence of then president of Ireland Éamonn de Valera.

'I was trying to get my thoughts together to see what I'd say. I didn't say very much. I don't agree with all this speech-making: All the county wants and all the captain wants to do is to get the cup and show it to the supporters,' says Frankie.

Once everything died down, the team made its way slowly to the outskirts at Malahide where a meal was given to them by the Waterfordmen's Assocation at 7 p.m. The specially printed menu features the full line-out of the team on one side with the menu on the other. The whole thing is in Irish and they obviously started their print run before the team changes were announced for the replay, as I have one copy with the team of the drawn game and one with the correct line-up. My dad clearly passed around the menu for signing to his team-mates.

Frank Lee, a society columnist with the *Evening Herald,* was amongst the press corps at the Grand Hotel that night. In his 'Going Places' column, he captures the exuberance of the evening:

Beating Kilkenny is worth two All-Irelands, Matt Maloney said triumphantly. Matt is secretary of the most over-worked Waterford Reception Committee. That remark is not meant incivilly. It is only a statement of fact: 1938, 1948, 1957 and twice this year. 'May I quote you?' I asked. 'In heavy type,' said Matt…. Kilkenny has long been a Waterford bogey. And yesterday the bogey was well and truly laid. Hence the particularly intense jubilation… The London–Irish party to the number of 30 or so joined the Waterford revellers and in their good fortune. And squeezing the last sweet drops of reminiscence from a splendid day the entire party was listening raptly to a recording of the last, fateful 10 minutes of play. As if to intensify the rapture of it all they ran a colour film of the 1957 game. 'You may think this is something,' said Matt, 'but it is nothing to what will happen in Waterford to-morrow. You should go down.' And maybe I shall do just that very thing.

Outside the hotel that evening, eager autograph hunters were swarming and the bonfires had been blazing that night all across County Waterford. In the unseasonably warm air, the county's highlands were ablaze with fires flaring along an 80-kilometre arc from Waterford city to Tallow.

'In the county capital great crowds moved through the city, waving blue and white flags, shaking rattlers and drumming on tin cans and empty barrels,' described an *Irish Press* reporter. 'First of the returning excursion trains were greeted exploding fog signals and blasts from ships' sirens. Up to a late hour a huge bonfire on Mount Misery, the 300ft cliff overlooking the city was being fed by tar barrels.'

The next day, the cavalcade of cars carrying the victorious team arrived in Waterford. Indeed, the fire brigade had had to quell the blaze on Mount Misery, which had grown to threaten nearby houses and buildings, but there was no dampening of the joy of the crowds in the Déise County. An estimated 40,000 people jammed the route of the open-top lorry to which the team was transferred after arriving in the city. This was how the *Irish Press* described the celebratory scenes on its front page:

> Waterford went wild last night as its hurler heroes came home from their great victory over Kilkenny in the All-Ireland senior final replay at Croke Park on Sunday. Ships'

sirens and train whistles heralded their arrival and jubilant flag-waving crowds escorted the team in a torchlight procession to a civic reception in the City Hall.

In the *Irish Independent*, a report of the team's arrival in Waterford, complete with photos, stands next to a larger piece with the headline 'In Seven Years 67,000 People left the Land.' But Waterford that evening was a recession-free zone:

> A dense mass of people filled the 700ft. Suir Bridge across which the All-Ireland trophy was carried aloft from the neighbouring Noreside county, and extended along the quays to the City Hall, where the team and officials were accorded a civic reception by the mayor Ald. R. Jones, City Manager Sean O'Giollain and members of the corporation.

There was to be another civic reception in Dungarvan, followed by weeks of celebration when the coveted cup was taken on a tour of all the schools in the county and all the towns and villages during the evenings. Within a week of their All-Ireland victory, Waterford were back on the field of action again – this time against Wexford in the National League. They won easily on a scoreline of 6-10 to 2-7.

My father came back to Tallow 'in the early hours of Tuesday morning', as the *Dungarvan Leader* reported. In those pre-mobile-phone days, the bonfires were lit and the crowd gathered in Tallow to welcome back their famous resident. At the end of an eight-hour vigil, the crowd had thinned somewhat, but there were still enough people to welcome him when he arrived at 4.30 a.m., whereupon he was carried shoulder-high to his recently purchased house in Chapel Street.

As the hype of victory died down, one wondered what was next for Waterford. The victory seems to have been down to a unique coming together of individuals – team, trainer, selectors and county board – that was somewhat unusual and the hope was that this spirit could be built upon and ensure more All-Irelands over the coming years. It was a hope that would not see fruition and one that was well-summarised in *Deiseach*'s column in the *Waterford News & Star* on October 13th:

> In the midst of all the celebrations and back-slapping, let's steady ourselves or a moment and look towards the future. 1959 will go into history as the greatest year in Waterford

hurling, the culmination of three years of striving on the part of players, selectors and county officials, a study in cooperation which has rarely been equalled and, certainly, never surpassed. All that is true and honour to the men – particularly the players – who brought it about. But, with the same will to win, with equal and sustained concentration on victory and with that zeal and unity of purpose, without which there is no success, 1959, far from being the end, can be made the prelude to an era of undreamed glory for the Decies.

CHAPTER 14

MY FATHER ON FAMILY HOLIDAY

From some time in the late 1970s until the mid-1980s, we had a caravan. We actually had two, but the first one was a little too big and too difficult to tow around, so my parents down-sized to a more compact Sprite model, which was purchased from friends from Enniskillen. It was a six-berth caravan that sat on the concrete back yard of our home and we loved it. As a treat (and if we were allowed), we would go and spend a night in it for the considerable adventure value that it offered even when stationary. It was fabulous.

Every year, there was a pattern of going to Lahinch on the Clare coast with the caravan. If childhood memories are supposed to be bathed in brilliant sunshine, the truth is that in my memories of holidays in Lahinch, that quality is distinctly lacking. I think we always managed to coincide our trips there with the arrival of a wet cold frontal weather system that lingered with a miserable persistence. But my parents both loved Lahinch and County Clare. Everywhere, they found people trusting, welcoming and honest.

Lahinch itself was a very small place at that time. This was long before developers and the surfing fraternity had discovered it (although we did appreciate Lahinch's big rolling waves for the 'jumping into' qualities that they held). In fact, my mother recalls that any shopping for basics such as milk or a newspaper would have to be done in the nearby village of Ennistymon. Here, my dad came across something that he had never seen in County Waterford – newspapers left in a barrel for people to take, trusting that in doing so, they would also make sure to drop the appropriate amount of money into the appropriate slot.

The owner of the camp site would, in my mother's words, 'greet us with an open mind and an open heart'. When it was time to pay for their stay, she would ask them: 'When did ye arrive?', trusting that my father's answer would be an honest one. There was one light in the campsite, which was located outside a shed, in which was housed the toilet and a tap with cold running water. We, the happy children, played contentedly in the fantastic bumps and hollows of the field. In the evening, we would walk the short walk into the village on our own and walk back again, often in the company of Donie Nealon's children. Despite the fact that they used to play on opposing sides (he for Tipperary and my dad for Waterford), Donie was a good friend of my dad's. They knew each other from their hurling days in the 1950s and 1960s, as well both being prominent members of the coaching staff at the Gormanstown training camps. In another example of the unreliability of happy memories, my mother recalls meeting the Nealons on a regular basis, but when I asked Donie about it, he insisted that it was just the once and that on that occasion, it was they who were in a caravan and we who were in a B&B.

For some reason (maybe it was the rain), my memories of the holidays in Lahinch are fond, but very hazy. I remember rain and mud, taking my father's hand and shivering in the morning as we made our way to the sanitary block, washing in cold water, jumping in the huge waves, sitting listening and laughing in the caravan at night, making friends with children from Slough in England (where they make the Mars bars) and who were always being called home to their caravan to 'come and get your bread and jam'. I remember feeling bored in a museum in the Burren and tugging my mother's leg to get her attention and then getting the fright of my life (literally) when the person whom I had assumed to be my mother turned out to be a bearded man who had worn his hair fashionably long for the seventies.

I also remember making friends with a boy from Gort in Galway who was on holiday there too and I remember how, typically enough, he was far more excited to learn that my dad had been on an All-Ireland winning team than I was. Where was his medal? At home. Had I seen it?

Yes, I think so. Were you allowed to touch it? What was it like? I really wasn't sure and I recall his obsession with this medal getting me down a little, as I stared with some envy from the sideline while my father showed the awe-struck child some of the basic skills in hurling and patiently fielded his many questions.

The family holiday that stands out the most for me was one we took near Dingle on the Corca Dhuibhne Peninsula in Kerry. It was around 1982. This time, the caravan stayed at home. I'm not sure why – maybe the family leaders had grown tired of hauling the caravan on long journeys and had limited themselves to the relatively short occasional jaunts to Ardmore. We stayed in a farmhouse with a sloping floor which was a two-storey house at one end and a single-storey house at the other. As if that in itself wasn't wonderful enough, there was also a fabulous cove with a sandy beach just a short walk across a couple of fields, where very few people besides ourselves seemed to go and it was overlooked by the ruin of a castle which my mother told me was used in a film called *Ryan's Daughter*.

It was a week of continental levels of calm, unrelenting sunshine, so Dad was in his element; bare-chested from dawn to dusk, he divided his time between sitting on the strand reading the newspaper, going for a swim early in the morning with us and sitting reading the newspaper by the house. We also went for car trips, visiting Dingle and various other beauty spots in the vicinity.

A few years later, my parents had sold the caravan. The oldest siblings – Patricia and Seán – had out-grown the family holiday scene in any case. After a trip to France on their own, my parents had fallen for the country in a big way and the next family holiday was to be in a mobile home on the Vendée coast. This pattern continued for a number of years. There were certain items that went everywhere with us in the car. First and foremost, there were the hurleys and balls and the second most important item was a large bag of Irish potatoes. The latter were always to be purchased on the day of departure and had to be from Mick O'Keefe's. The beaches of Les Sables d'Olonne were wide and flat and very conducive for playing hurling. The sight of the ancient Irish game being played on the strand drew curious stares from French onlookers. It also drew the attention of fellow Irish citizens within the vicinity – of which there were always some – and even in France, we were treated to the familiar sight of someone coming up to my dad after recognising him in action with hurley and ball and standing talking to him for some time.

Although my father was a fluent Irish speaker, he never got around to mastering another language, apart from the Latin he learned in school. It's a shame because he was a person who was always eager to keep learning and improving generally and he also had the very important quality (from a language-learning point of view) of not being afraid to have a go at expressing himself in another language. Coupled with his sense of fun and his talent for mimicry, I'm sure he would have quickly become fluent in whatever language he put his mind to learning if he had given it the time.

During our trips to France, he would rely on the secondary-school French of myself or my older sister Annette to assist him when he wanted to know how to say something. Later on, both my parents took some French classes to try to get a better handle on communicating. Lack of time both in learning it and in the quantity of time spent in the country mitigated against them making too much progress. There were some words that I remember my father retaining very well for their comedic value. Chief amongst them was *un petit peu* (a little bit), which Dad found amusing to pronounce *a petty poo*. Nevertheless, he would make superb efforts to explain to curious French people all about the intricacies of hurling using only the words *irlandais* and *hurling*, some improvised miming and noises that he made with his mouth, often with his tongue sticking out.

After learning how to say *Je suis irlandais*, he would use it whenever and wherever possible when in France. Each time, he'd hunch up his shoulders, open his eyes wide, spread his hands out with his palms facing upwards and deliver the line with all the emotion, feeling and Gallic drama and exaggerated deep-toned accent that he could possibly muster in a loud voice. Shop assistants, people giving directions, camp site officials, waiters in restaurants and petrol attendants – they all met Ned Power and heard him say that he was Irish in their language and in a manner more theatrical than any of them would say such a mundane thing themselves. They were all charmed and impressed, I think. It always got a smile and a warm reaction, even though they must have thought that they were dealing with an Irishman who had been watching a little too much of Maurice Chevalier.

After my mother joined him in retirement in 1997, there was more travelling to be done. By this stage, Dad's mobility was beginning to suffer a little, but this didn't stop him from getting to enjoy the warm North African sunshine of Tunisia. They also went to Jersey – the scene of their honeymoon over three decades previously, joined by my mother's sister Maria and her husband John, who used to often travel with them on holiday.

One of his last swims in the sea was at the Lido di Jesolo on the Adriatic coast in Italy near Venice. He was on holiday with my mother and his brother Brendan had also accompanied them and at this point in his life, he was frail and he bruised extremely easily. It was during the evening and Dad had decided to go for a dip in the warm sea. But the cross winds and the waves were rising and he was being increasingly pushed across the beach towards the pier wall. Another passing Irishman who happened to be on the beach, jumped in and helped to rescue my father from the surf, where Dad was hanging on grimly to a rock. He had sustained a fair bit of bruising and cuts from his battle with the tide which, by all accounts he most definitely would not have won had it not been for the intervention of some help. He even had to get some hospital treatment involving bandages, but he still managed to seek out an Irish pub with satellite GAA for a hurling match the next day.

Typical of Dad, though, he was too proud to admit how close he had come to disaster and he just said 'I'm fine… a bit of bruising, that's all.' It was only in conversation some months later with my mother's sister Maria that he admitted – only to her – that he had had a very close shave that day.

CHAPTER 15

THE EARLY SIXTIES

The year 1960 must have felt like a great year for my father, for Waterford, for Tallow. The All-Ireland victory of 1959 had been tinged with sadness at the death of both his father in May and my mother's father in October.

He was an All-Ireland champion who was on his way to a once-in-a-lifetime trip to New York and he was getting married. Even the economic climate of the country was changing. The space race was well and truly on, with its latest records and achievements appearing in large block capitals across the front pages of all the national papers.

My father had just made his first acquisition in buying a house on Chapel Street, which was to be the family home for the next seven years.

The Waterford team had finished 1959 off in the style of the team to beat with an eye to future All-Ireland glory, by giving Wexford a sound thrashing in their next league game and by drawing with Kilkenny.

The 1960 championship campaign, however, was to be short-lived. In June 1960, the 'unbeatable' Tipperary, who had been so humiliated by Waterford less than a year earlier, were waiting in the long grass for the confident All-Ireland champions. This time, it was the men from the

Premier County who had a goal-spree. Waterford went down by ten points on a scoreline of 6-7 to 2-9.

They did get to go to New York, however. This was quite a treat for all the lads on the team. Nowadays, teams not only travel after winning an All-Ireland final, but they travel abroad if they lose, for functions of an Irish society somewhere in the world or even for training sessions to the southern half of Europe. Back then, the tradition of an All-Ireland winning team being brought on a foreign trip had not been established so it was with great excitement that they headed off across the Atlantic Ocean – on an aeroplane, no less! In an era where Irish people fly to New York to go shopping, it might not seem like the grand adventure that it was, but in 1960 foreign travel was not the *de rigeur* luxury that it is today and for someone from Ireland to fly to New York for a holiday and come back again within weeks to tell the tale was quite something.

It was, in fact, the Waterfordmen's Association in New York that had organised and paid for the trip, but the journey still had to be approved by GAA Congress in Dublin.

'I had to go to Congress to ask permission,' says Frankie Walsh, 'because we had to get official expenses. They were offering to put us up in a hotel. We had a meal allowance and a laundry allowance… the Waterfordmen's Association looked after us brilliantly.'

As a pupil of my father's at the time, Billy Sheehan remembers the unheard-of excitement that was involved in the New York trip. 'It was such a rarity to meet someone who was actually there!' said Billy. 'He would tell us all about it in great detail in school; we'd be asking him questions, and of course he'd have all the accents down to a tee.'

A few days before they went to the USA, they went to London to play in a challenge match in Britain's premier soccer stadium Wembley against their All-Ireland rivals Kilkenny. Kilkenny won the match, as Larry Guinan remembers, but he did score two goals on that day.

'It's something I pride in,' he smiles, 'because it's often asked in pub quizzes to this day: "Who was the only Waterford man to score two goals in Wembley?" '

The team was billeted at the Manhattan Hotel for the week, during which the programme consisted of sight-seeing, playing a couple of matches and a good deal of free time for the players. One of the highlights of the trip was a visit to the restaurant of Jack Dempsey. Dempsey had been world heavyweight boxing champion a few decades previously and was still a major sports star and hailed as one of the best boxers of all time. Austin Flynn overheard a receptionist at the hotel talk about a 'Mr Dempsey'. He approached her and found out that it was indeed the famous Jack Dempsey who was in his restaurant. He got Larry Guinan and together they went upstairs to find my dad and Waterford team-mate Donal Whelan already there with a certain Old IRA veteran known as Fox Greaney and his wife – all in the company of the famous boxer. Together they got their photo taken.

As a child, I used to love leafing through all the photos of the New York trip and that group shot with my dad standing next to a tanned, US-fed Jack Dempsey (who, according to Frankie Walsh, had hands a multiple of the size of an average man's) was one of my favourites. It also came with a miniature pair of boxing gloves that were pre-signed by Dempsey. His signature, I'm sure, was probably printed onto these little souvenir trinkets and turned out by the hundred. But I loved them – that and the model of the Statue of Liberty. I asked my dad on a number of occasions if I could have them. But he clearly treasured them just as much and preferred to hold onto them.

Every day during his trip to New York, my father wrote a postcard home to his fiancée. She still has them as a treasured souvenir. They make poignant reading, always addressing my mother affectionately, using Gaelic terms of endearment such as 'A ghrá' or 'A stór'. Most of them are of views of New York sights – Times Square with traffic such as exists only in Cuba now, the Empire State Building, the Statue of Liberty. There's also one featuring a cartoon of a man warning against marriage. In the message on the reverse side, my dad apologises but confesses that he found it too funny and he 'just couldn't resist it'.

The men had plenty of free time and they went off in small groups, generally speaking. Some had relatives in the city, including Philly Grimes – who had actually spent some years in New York before coming back to Waterford – who would go to visit his uncle in Brooklyn.

*   *   *

My parents were married on the 11th of August, 1960 at the Catholic Church in Castlelyons, County Cork, which was my mother's home parish. Jersey in the Channel Islands was where they went for their honeymoon and their first home was the terraced house that my dad bought a year or so earlier in Chapel Street. Their first child – my sister Patricia – was born to them nine months later in May of 1961.

The early 1960s was a time when my father was rearing a young family, but it was also a time of great activity in his GAA career. Having narrowly missed out on being elected to the Western Board of Waterford GAA in 1960, he began to put more and more energy into coaching hurling and football in Tallow. Having established his home and family there, he also became a member of the Tallow GAA club in the early 1960s and was lining out for them on the junior team that they had at the time.

Waterford's golden era wasn't finished yet, though. In the 1961 championship, they exited for the second year in a row at the Munster semi-final stage – this time going down to Cork on a scoreline of 5-7 to 2-7. To make matters worse, my father was substituted in that game. When you're taken out of a team at the age of 31, it's always liable to be a bit of a struggle to get back into the team and it was taken as read that my dad's inter-county adventure was at an end.

The next year – 1962 – Waterford got through the first round of the Munster championship against Clare without much difficulty, beating them by 23 points to 9. My father didn't play in that game. In the next match – the Munster semi-final – however, they were up against old enemies and hurling aristocrats Cork. Dad got a late call to the team and was one of the stars of the show as Waterford overcame their illustrious rivals and made it to their first Munster final in three years.

It was, by all accounts, a tough and furious game played in brilliant sunshine in Thurles. A lot of neutral observers had been putting down the failures of Waterford over the previous few years to their propensity for 'nice guy hurling', that they weren't as prepared as Cork or Tipperary for the rough and tumble of championship hurling – which was, I think, considerably rougher than it is today. But the Waterford team that day was in determined mood. By the end of the match, three of their star players had been sidelined, each one receiving an injury more grave than the previous player: Jim Irish with a deep gash in his shoulder blade, Tom Cheasty with a broken collar bone and Frankie Walsh, who had suffered a blow to his wrist that had broken his ulna in three places.

The newspapers were superfluous in their praise of Waterford's performance, none more so than *Déiseach* in the *Waterford News & Star*:

> The date, July 8, 1962, is forever emblazoned in letters of gold in Waterford's hurling story… Nothing we have achieved in the past surpassed it: nothing we may achieve in the future can dim its glory. It was Munster Championship hurling at

Have Another One, Christy!

Dad attempting to clear his lines with Christy Ring hot on his heels, circa 1961.

The Field

At the official opening of the GAA Field in Tallow, 1963, (L ro R) Bill Sheehan, Jimmy Cunningham, Donal Whelan, Mossy Pollard, Rodger Dwan, Dad, Mick Curley and Ned Condon.

Gormanstown, 1965

Dad front & centre; his first year of Gormanstown, with a course team.

Ballinasloe, 1966
Dad & Deise team-mate Austin Flynn line out for Munster in a 1966 Railway Cup clash with Connacht.

Gormanstown, 1970
Dad, Fr Tommy Maher and Des Nealon "in camp" on the steps of Gormanstown College, 1970.

1971 under 14 selection

This panel completed a county final double in hurling and football, but what is even more remarkable about this group is that no fewer than seven of them went on to play senior hurling for Waterford; namely, Pat Daly, Kieran Ran, Connie Curley, Mickey Curley, Timmy Sheehan, Raymond O'Brien and Stephen Curley.

Breakthrough Team

*The Intermediate Tallow Hurling team that broke into the senior ranks by winning the Waterford Intermediate title, 1974.
My father is in the middle row, third from left.*

Friendly Rivals
My dad (left) & Tony Mansfield shake hands as coaches of rival teams Tallow and Abbeyside/Ballinacourty, post-match in Cappoquin, 1976.

Speak Softly with a Clenched Fist
Dad delivering the half-time message to the Tallow junior team, county final, 1982. Tallow won.

1980 Champions

The Tallow senior hurling team that won the 1980 Waterford county final against Dunhill. Dad is second from right.

A Man who Loved the Sun
In his element on family holiday, Kerry, July 1983.

Wedding Chauffeur
The father of the bride making a joke to camera. My sister Patricia is the one in the wedding dress. May 1984.

its furious, exhilarating best. The exchanges were hectic in the extreme, and men vied with one another in demonstrations of courage, determination and fighting spirit. It was a game made memorable by the uncertainty of the hour and by absolute ferocity with which the issue was disputed. Through this testing, fiery hour, Waterford fought like men inspired and, in the end, they had triumphed not only over Cork, but over a combination of circumstances and events that would have dominated men of lesser heart.

In singling out individual performances, first on *Déiseach*'s list was my father:

> What of Ned Power, the man who came back to record his greatest triumph at the scene of his failure a year ago? Power was a man inspired on Sunday. In the air, on the ground, Power was dynamic. His was a decisive contribution to a wonderful victory.

> Remember the man in the Munster final of '59 and in the All-Irelands of the same year? I do not propose to spoil your contemplation of that picture. I will say no more about the man who came back from the wilderness to share in a mighty game.

That was also the day of that famous photograph of my father jumping high into the air to catch the ball – a picture which told so much about the match and about hurling in one single frame. Frankie Walsh, the man who had to sit out much of the second half after a multiple fracture of his arm, worked for a company called Measurex. One of its clients was a paper mill in Borlänge, Sweden. In 1988, Frankie and another Waterford colleague were in Borlänge carrying out contract work in the paper mill. The company, according to Frankie was one of the biggest paper mills in Europe, supplying newsprint for various titles all over the continent. When he and his colleague walked into the smart reception area of the premises, they saw a familiar sight: There, hanging on the wall, was Louis McMonagle's iconic photograph. The manager at the mill knew nothing about hurling but, amongst the many thousands of photographs of the hundreds of newspapers he dealt with, this picture had struck a chord with him. The two men couldn't believe their eyes and breathlessly let the receptionist know that one of them was actually playing in that bizarre-looking sport depicted in the photograph. The manager was informed and many awe-struck questions about hurling followed. They were, according to Frankie, 'wined and dined' for the rest of the week.

But that furiously intense match had weakened the Waterford team and they were to receive a sobering lesson in championship hurling at the hands of their bogeymen from Tipperary on August 6th. They were beaten by a margin of 20 points on a scoreline of 5-14 to 2-3. Waterford was to get some modicum of revenge later the same year when they surprised Tipperary by beating them in the Oireachtas Cup final in October. That particular competition isn't running any more. It was one of my dad's most treasured medals, distinctive with its flaming torch emblem on the front. It is also, incidentally, the only medal that Christy Ring never won.

The year 1963 was to be Waterford's last appearance in an All-Ireland final until 2008. Four years after their triumph in 1959, the team was now on an upward trajectory again, having experienced a good year in '62, despite the heavy defeat in the Munster final.

My parents became parents for the second time on May 23rd, 1963. That evening, my father dropped my mother to the Bons Secours Hospital in Cork before continuing his journey to Clonmel, where he lined out for Waterford in a pre-championship tournament match against familiar foes Tipperary. In common with most expectant fathers of that era, his presence at the birth of his child was neither expected nor requested. While Dad was playing hurling, my mother's mother Julia O'Flynn was babysitting for my sister Patricia, who was two years old.

My grandmother, it must be said, idolised my father. To her, he was as perfect a son-in-law as you could get: he was handsome, charming, diligent, hard-working, healthy, he had a reputable steady occupation and fine standing in the community and he wasn't a drinker. She readily forgave any of Dad's transgressions and would plead with my mother to do likewise, if and when the occasion called for it.

That evening, Julia had a very anxious wait. She had her hands full looking after a little toddler and her daughter was in hospital hoping to give birth again. The hours ticked by. Ned's game was at seven, which meant it would be over at eight, which meant that, failing incident, her son-in-law would be home no later than half past nine or ten o'clock.

As ten o'clock came and went, my grandmother began to feel certain that Dad must have visited the hospital. The sooner he was back from there, the greater the likelihood was that everything had gone smoothly. At eleven o'clock, my father's Ford Anglia pulled up on the street outside. Granny rushed to the door, opened it and stood there awaiting some news from my father. He was calmly removing hurleys and gear from the boot.

'Well?' she finally said. 'Is there any news?'

My father looked startled for a moment.

'What? Oh yes… We got beaten! And I broke my best hurley off Mackey McKenna.'

'No, no… What about Gretta? Did you hear any news about Gretta and the baby?'

My father, nonplussed and with complete confidence in a successful birth and in everyone being in good health, just said something like: 'I'm sure it's fine. Sure, we'll give the hospital a ring there.'

He rang the hospital and was informed that everything was fine, that he was now the proud father of a baby boy and that both mother and child were doing well. He looked to my grandmother and said: 'There you are – a baby boy. They're both grand.'

The news that my brother Seán – the first son and heir of the great Ned Power – was born to the world was greeted with great excitement by some in Tallow. The local parish priest Canon Flynn ran down the street most of the length of Tallow as soon as he heard to let hackney driver and former Waterford All-Ireland goalkeeper Mick Curley know.

There are mothers-in-law who would not think much of such a performance from their son-in-law, who would look with annoyance and frustration on such a casual attitude, trusting that divine providence will ensure that everything will be alright. But not my grandmother. That exchange only served to reinforce her heroic image of my dad.

On the field of play, Waterford were having a good year and building on the promise they had showed in 1962. My dad was having a real Indian summer end to his inter-county career and his place on the team was as assured as it had ever been over the previous six years of playing for Waterford. His philosophy of constant improvement – something that wasn't shared by all players, even those at the top level – was paying off and he was regarded by many as the finest goalkeeper in the country.

They played Limerick in the Munster semi-final (an unusual opponent to find at the semi-final stage during those years when Cork and Tipperary were so dominant) on July 7th and won by a close margin of two points. Their next opponents, on July 28th, were Tipperary. These were the championship bogeymen of Waterford. They hadn't beaten them in the championship since their emphatic and unexpected victory over them in the Munster semi-final of 1959. After all their heroics in recent campaigns, the feeling was that of determination and, perhaps that if they could just beat Tipperary, then a second deserved All-Ireland was on the cards. It was not to be Tipperary's day. Not only were they beaten by Waterford, but their minor team also lost out to Limerick in the earlier match. They came back 'hurling magnificently in the second half after being in arrears' according to Peadar O'Brien in the *Irish Press*, who also heaped praise on my dad's performance: 'Power, all through, was soundness personified in the Waterford goal. He got most help from a tireless Flynn at full-back, Larry Guinan, Tom Cunningham and Jim Irish.'

'Wonderful Triumph For Waterford,' was the headline on the sports page of the *Cork Examiner*, which spoke of a quality game in which no goals were scored between the All-Ireland and Munster champions (Tipperary) and the Oireachtas and League champions (Waterford). The report also spoke of the delight of the Waterford players at the end of the match, which they won 0-11 to 0-8:

> They had beaten Tipperary in the championship. This was a solid irrefutable thing, the memory of last year's final defeat was erased and they proclaimed their delight with an excess of exuberance as though this was their first and not their fifth provincial title. And when they write this result in the records, in addition to the victories of 1938, '48, '57 and '59, they can cherish it as one of, if not their greatest, championship final wins.

In the final, they were playing familiar foes: For the third time in as many All-Ireland finals, Kilkenny stood in their way. Looking at the pictures of my dad and all the others, there is a distinctive difference between them and the 1959 ones. All the players are a little older, with many of them having got married, settled down and put on a bit of weight. But there's also a certain grizzled, serious and battle-hardened look about them – they look like men who have been to war and seen things they'd rather not talk about.

The core of the team that won the All-Ireland was still there and it was something of a mystery to many analysts why this exceptional, tight-knit team hadn't managed to win more All-Irelands than their haul of just one over the previous six seasons, while their neighbour Tipperary had racked up three, with Wexford and Kilkenny having got one title each during the same period.

Waterford Must Be My Choice, *trumpets Mick Dunne with confidence in the Irish Press of the Friday before the big day.* It takes Croke Park to bring out the best in Waterford. So I wrote after their Oireachtas final triumph last October and this would have been my theme again had I reported their victory in the National League 'home' final in May. And because I believe Croke Park can have the same beneficial effect on them again, I am prepared to overlook their relatively unimpressive performance in the Munster final and bank on them to win Sunday's All-Ireland final….

It is indeed one of the coincidences and quirks of hurling fate that on each of the three most recent occasions these counties have qualified for the All-Ireland final they have done so together…. Furthermore, these two neighbours, who have so many close connections in social and sporting life, are not very far apart in the brands of hurling they play. Both play a stylish, polished type of hurling that is spectacular and thrilling to watch. The only difference, to my mind, is that Waterford have added to their style just a little of the traditional Munster grit and doggedness. And this has become more pronounced as their determination and zeal has grown over the years this team has been together. Yet, no hurling side that I have seen have displayed such a devastatingly effective cohesion. The fact that so many of these players have been together for so long accounts for this. Through nearly seven years in top-class senior hurling they have consolidated their splendid team-work until now they move with a rhythm that is almost instinctive. They deploy the ball bewilderingly at times and they use the open spaces and create the extra man with telling effect.

J.D. Hickey in the *Irish Independent* the same day concurs: 'FORM POINTS TO A WATERFORD WIN', says the headline. After assessing the merits of both in a long piece, he points to a lack of firepower in the Kilkenny attack (with the exception of their new star player Eddie Keher) and notes that 'It also weighs with me that All-Ireland winning sides do not grow up over-night, as it were, and I feel that Kilkenny are still in the process of development.'

The *Waterford News & Star* gave a three-page spread to the match, featuring photos showing the team training, drinking tea in the dressing room and there's even one of my dad getting a massage from team masseur Jack Furlong. In an emotionally charged piece, *Déiseach* appeals:

> Yes, a County goes with you; a County waits to greet your return. Go to Croke Park, fight the good fight with all that is in you and come back to us champions of All-Ireland. You have the ability, in hurling brilliance you are unmatched. Your will to win has been demonstrated over and over again. This is your hour, your date with destiny. You must win for Portlairge. The mantle of champions will fit you well. To Croke Park and victory!

The match set the record as the highest-scoring All-Ireland hurling at that time but Waterford were not able to cope with a Kilkenny team that played well and, in particular, the aforementioned newcomer Eddie Keher. Keher, who went on to become one of the all-time greats in the game of hurling, set a very high standard in that match, scoring 14 points of his team's final tally of 4-17. Live television was now a reality in Ireland and this was the second All-Ireland to be seen by the nation's television owners, so many thousands more got the opportunity to witness the match and Keher's display, who became a good friend of my father's and was always one of my dad's favourite players.

As for my father, he had an unhappy day all round.

'He told me himself that the biggest disappointment of his inter-county playing career was losing the All-Ireland final of 1963,' remembers Séamus O'Brien. In the *Irish Press* the following day, Padraig Puirseal describes the action and how the tide began to turn in Kilkenny's favour during the first half and my father's role in the sequence of events:

First, following a goal-mouth mix-up, blond Tom Walsh from Thomastown shot through a whole mound of players (they had crashed to earth in the Railway square) for Kilkenny's first goal.

The stands seemed to rock to the cheering that then surged out not in a single roar, but in great waves, almost a crashing surf of sound that was stilled to shocked silence seconds later as goalkeeper Ned Power, policing a slow-moving ball that he expected to pass outside the post chased it into his own net, for the most tragic score ever in an All-Ireland final.

Looking at the video of the match, my father is moving slowly and lacking in his usual agility when that ball rolled in after being struck by Tom Murphy and bouncing into the net off the butt of the upright. It turns out that he was in great pain, having fractured a rib in an earlier exchange. He had called to be taken off, but clearly the selectors didn't quite appreciate until the half-time break just how seriously hurt he was. Percy Flynn came on as substitute goalkeeper for the second half, during which the team rallied but without success and the winning margin was close in the end, at just three points.

Most analysts described the game in glowing terms, including Prince Rainier and Princess Grace of Monaco, who, according to the *Irish Press*, 'were said to have been thrilled the game and marvelled at the skill and speed of the players. They had never seen anything like it before.'

'Fast, almost too exciting… It's marvellous,' the princess is quoted as saying in the *Irish Independent*, which also notes that she 'worried about the danger to players and surprised at the same time at the remarkably few instances of injuries.'

Part of the intense disappointment that my father felt on that day, along with the rest of the team, was the knowledge that the core of this team was an ageing one, with most of their most reliable stars now being 30 or more. Dad himself was within a few months of his 34th birthday and must have known, watching the 21-year-old Keher fly around the park and rack up his high score that day, that his body was getting to the stage where it wasn't going to be able to cope with the demands of such intensity as championship hurling demanded.

He would play on with Waterford for another three years, but 1963 was to be a landmark date in Waterford hurling for all the wrong reasons: It was to be the year of their last League title for 44 years and the year of their last appearance in an All-Ireland final for another 45.

CHAPTER 16

MY FATHER, THE GOLFER

When exactly my father started playing golf, I don't know. I do know that it was my mother who played golf long before he did. As the family began to grow, she played less golf and, as Dad's hurling career waned, the more into the less physically demanding sport of golf he got. One thing that did surprise me, though, was the discovery that it was not regarded by the GAA as a foreign sport. Golf is widely believed to have started in Scotland in the 12th century, but I'm certain that it didn't start in Ireland. The 'ban' didn't cover sports like golf. It only covered team sports.

But back to the foreign-but-never-banned game of golf: I never got to experience playing a round of golf with my father. In this, I'm alone in my family; all the others have played and continue to play golf. His local golf club was Lismore – a rival and ancient settlement 8 km from Tallow – and I remember him taking me there once as a child. It was a typical memory of me accompanying my father and everyone stopping to talk to him. To use a golfing term, that sort of an outing with my father was par for the course. At first he would be all attentive, taking me by the hand and listening to what I had to say. But invariably, the next person we'd run into on the street, in the butcher's, at the supermarket or at the golf club would take his attention from me to discuss some matter or other that may have revolved around GAA. Then I'd sort-of tune out and look around me.

On this particular trip to the golf course, I remember finding myself in that same situation, only this time I was in unfamiliar territory. I had picked up on the strange expressions such as 'birdie', 'par' and 'handicap' and I wanted to know what they all meant. I suppose (like any young boy), I wanted to inhabit some of the more unknown domains in my father's universe.

Whatever age I was, I found the whole game and the people who populated it mysterious, pointless and intimidating. That first impression must have made a deep impact on my psyche because I am the only one of the entire basic family unit of the Tallow Powers who has never played golf.

Even when I was living in Bantry, I came very very close to joining the local club and investing in the game's awkward-sized accoutrements. But I just couldn't bring myself to get up on that Sunday morning and drag myself onto the golf course. I'm convinced to this day that there was something in that first childhood experience of golfing that gave me a profound, almost genetic aversion to golf courses – not unlike that unfortunately demonically possessed child in the *Damian* horror film series, who hissed and fretted like the devil himself in the back of the car every time his parents tried to bring him anywhere near a church.

My father had no such hang-ups and he loved his golf. He used to love the fresh air and the exercise of it, the banter and the very soft-core betting that he and his golfing buddies would partake in, the lost balls and the comments that would define and characterise each opponent and playing partner, depending on their reaction to how a shot went.

According to my father, there were two types of shot in golf, which were defined by what one said immediately after hitting, walloping or stroking the ball. These were 'Shit!' and ''Twill do!' The first one was when the ball went hopelessly astray and the second one when it managed to stay within bounds. A lot of golfers (apparently) like a good moan about their misfortune or lack of form, but there was no time for moaning in my father's book and he was, as one commentator described him (okay, it was my brother Barry), 'sometimes infuriatingly positive'. He'd much prefer to say something like 'Never mind, the next one will be better' than moan about it.

The betting side of things never got serious in any way with him. He loved the challenge but didn't want things to get too silly. Usually, the bet involved the princely sum of one pound, for which he and another would do battle on Lismore's golf course on either a Sunday morning or some fine long summer evening.

Mick O'Grady was Dad's golfing partner for much of the time when I was growing up. This affable man was sometimes affectionately referred to as 'Ah… no!' by my father because that's what he was wont to say when his shot went astray. 'I got a pound from O'Grady this morning' was a regular phrase heard around the teatime table, where he'd be regaling us with the highlights of his golfing expedition, whether we listened attentively or not. 'I had a par on the 14th (the toughest hole on the course) and at the 17th and a birdie (if you don't mind!) at the 10th.' Even now, this stuff is largely gobbledygook to me and I would smile back blankly as he continued his complete run-down on his miraculous recovery at the 5th and how his partner had 'made a mess' on the same hole. I'd like to have shared his enthusiasm and fully understand why at the same time.

Mick O'Grady and himself played in competitions with the club too, and the highlight of all this was probably when they represented Lismore – apparently with some distinction too – at the Pierce Purcell Shield.

Another of his great golfing partners was Connie Ryan. Having played tennis and acted in plays together during my dad's early years in Tallow, it all came full circle when Connie took up golfing relatively late in life and began playing with my father in the 1990s.

Dad continued golfing as long as his body would allow him to. About two years before his death, he had just come out of hospital and his doctor had advised him not to play. 'Certainly not,' the surgeon had told my mother. 'His heart is weak and he is simply not able for a full round of golf.'

The trouble was that my dad could never see the point of going out for a game of golf and not completing the course. To him, I think that the very essence of golfing was to be able to complete the challenge, so retiring half-way, playing nine rounds or pulling out at any point before the full 18 was the sort of behaviour that my father would not tolerate. This had always been his belief as a golfer, and just because his legs were weak, his heart was dicky and he was into his mid-seventies, he wasn't going to change now.

Knowing this, my mother decided to talk to a friend of his and sometimes golfing partner Paddy Carry. She intimated to Paddy the gravity of the situation according the medical experts and that, under no circumstances should Ned play a full round of golf. His deteriorating physical condition simply wasn't up to it. Paddy agreed that he would take my dad out for a round. At around the 9th hole, the plan was that Paddy would say that he was a bit tired or that he had some other pressing engagement to which he really should attend. This would then give my father – who would surely be feeling the strain of things by that point – the optimum excuse to be able to retire from the day's golfing with his dignity intact.

On the day, my father set off early in the morning, happy to be heading out the door once more onto the green. My mother was expecting him back in the door at 2pm and had prepared some food for him (one interesting thing about my dad is that his ravenous appetite never wavered until right at the very end). By four o'clock, there was still no sign of the aged golfer and she was getting concerned. Finally, four fraught hours later at seven o'clock in the evening, she heard a car arriving outside and she went out to face what she feared might be an ambulance crew, a doctor or even Paddy Carry himself bearing some bad news. But it was my father who materialised at the door.

'What happened?' asked my startled mother.

'Oh, we got on fine,' my dad answered, nonchalantly.

'And what about Paddy Carry?' she asked, looking around for evidence of the missing golfing partner.

'That fellah!... Ol' eejit gave up at the ninth – said he was tired! I had to finish it with someone else. Imagine!'

CHAPTER 17

A COACHING CAREER

There has been much debate in recent years about the state of hurling in the country. Hurling is rated as one of the most skilful field games in the world. It takes a lot of training and practice in order to be able to field a competitive team and it's no coincidence that there are only a handful of counties in Ireland that are capable of winning an All-Ireland. Munster has the greatest concentration of hurling counties, with five of the six counties in the province all capable of achieving All-Ireland glory.

In Leinster, there are perhaps four out of their twelve counties up to that standard. In Connacht, there is one, while in Ulster – despite the fact that there are a number of very strong clubs in many pockets of the province – no county has ever won a senior All-Ireland title. On top of that, there are two counties which dominate the hurling scene far more than any others, namely Cork and Kilkenny, with the latter county having achieved an almost total dominance in recent years. This was recently (and personally for me as a Waterford man, excruciatingly painfully) illustrated with shocking clarity in the final of 2008 when Waterford were trounced by their neighbours in a record-breaking winning margin. On that same day, Kilkenny also won the minor title, adding to under-21 and camogie titles in the same year and thus completing a clean sweep of all the major hurling titles.

That so few dominate in one sport is not a good thing and it's an issue that hasn't yet been properly addressed by the GAA. There are the great hurling counties and then there the good hurling counties. Below that, there are many many counties where there is a hunger to learn and develop this game. It's at these levels that evangelical zeal is needed to bring the sport to the people and grow it so that it becomes an integral part of the culture of the county.

My father was one of these apostles – one who worked tirelessly to bring the game to as many people and as many counties as possible and to continue to examine and improve the game for his own benefit as well as for the benefit of those already considered to be brilliant hurlers.

During the course of a discussion on RTÉ radio in March, 2008 on the state of hurling in Ireland, former Offaly coach Diarmuid Healy underlined the fact that 'hurling and football are two totally different games. The only thing in common is that they're both run by the GAA. After that, they're totally different… and we need to set up separate structures in the GAA for hurling and football. There's no point in the same committee drawing up coaching regulations and coaching practices for both football and hurling.'

In the same interview, he went on to say that the greatest revolution in hurling was in the 1960s when a group of four that included Fr Tommy Maher, Donie Nealon, Des Ferguson and my dad 'came together, week after week, analysed the game, drew up the different aspects of the skills, how to implement them and so on. Then they approached Croke Park and said: "Look, we want to run coaching courses around the country." They said: "We've no problem with your idea, but you'll have to call it 'Instructional Courses'" because coaching was seen as professional.'

Looking back on those days now, it seems a rather ludicrous standpoint for the GAA to take, particularly in this age where inter-county and even club coaching have become a professional pastime. Here, after all, was a small dedicated group of people who were presenting the GAA with a green paper on the skills of hurling and who were proposing to promote the game all over the country and instil a love and a culture of the game in all those areas that were barren to the ancient Gaelic game. It was a proposal that was central to the core principles and aims of the organisation. It was the panacea on a plate but the GAA accepted it only cautiously under certain conditions. They were, it seems, worried where it all might lead to.

The organisation seems to be dogged by this sort of reticence for change and clarity of vision throughout its life. In one sense it's a good thing: I believe that professionalism in sport has become a corrupting influence in general. When you turn a pastime and joyful thing into a simple commodity, you end up with the situation such as exists in professional soccer today, where it's okay for foreign billionaires who know little about the game to take over clubs with a century-old tradition simply by virtue of the size of their wallets; where players of average standard are paid the equivalent of several years' salary in one week, even though they're only playing it because they love it, where fans are being forced to fork out prices for tickets to see their heroes play which will cost them half a week of their income; where private television companies are allowed to hijack the viewing rights above the heads of national broadcasters for whatever amount of cash they can cobble together and then turn around and bleed it off the hapless sports fan, who continues to hand over because he's left with no choice in the matter, watching overpaid millionaires cheat the referee as much as they can get away with.

All this corruption becomes so insidious that even those that award players with titles such as World Player of the Year fail to even notice that the winner is also on the take in the cheating game.

Whilst such a monstrous money machine will never be able to exist in GAA sports (the volume of people simply isn't there; the 'market', as the commodity brokers say, is simply too small), the semi-professionalism of the game today has already corrupted football, which is continuing to develop its own culture of cheating by faking injury.

Developing a culture of refining skills and honest competitiveness was what my father was all about. His contemporaries on the Gormanston course shared this philosophy with him.

I met with one of those Gormanston contemporaries at his home near Nenagh in County Tipperary. Donie Nealon was a Tipperary forward in the 1960s and played against my father many times. Both men had the utmost respect and friendship for one another. My dad always classed him as one of the most skilful and clean hurlers he had encountered.

From the directions he gave me over the phone, I found Donie's house easily enough – it was a bungalow set off the public road with an all-important but relatively discreet Tipperary flag flying from one of the pillars at the entrance. Donie and his wife gave me the warmest of welcomes. I hadn't met them since I was approximately four years old and they scrutinised my face for resemblance of my parents as they shook my hand. Over tea and snacks, Donie explained to me exactly how Gormanston had started.

It was, he says, an initiative that came, in the first instance, from the GAA president Alf Murray. Alf was an Armagh man who, like many Northern GAA members, had what one person described to me as a sort of commitment with a cutting edge that typifies a Northern GAA member. He had made it a goal to revive hurling throughout the country so that all the weaker counties would be able to at least field a team of minor B level within a time-frame of five years. A football skills training camp was already under way in Gormanston involving Jim McKeever of Derry and Joe Lennon of Down. It was very successful, so Murray wanted to do the same for hurling.

Donie Nealon, Father Tommy Maher of Kilkenny (who had trained the Kilkenny senior team unsuccessfully against Waterford in the 1959 All-Ireland and successfully against us in 1963) and Des 'Stitchy' Ferguson of Dublin (a former dual player for his native county and whose son Terry was an All-Star corner back for Meath) made up the original triumvirate appointed to run the Gormanston training camps.

'There was no such thing as formal coaching courses then,' Donie underlined to me. 'You might have been coached on an individual basis by your parent or your teacher, but official coaching in GAA games didn't exist…

'You would have a bit of a puck around – playing backs-and-forwards and that sort of thing. But there was no such thing as someone showing you the right way to take a sideline cut or take a free, for example.'

The three men – all teachers – were given a carte blanche to devise and run a coaching course, with the aforementioned proviso that the 'c' word was not mentioned and the term 'training' used in preference. This was all within a small budget and the idea of remuneration for their time didn't enter the equation; not that it mattered as all the men were only too happy and privileged to be carrying out such work.

During the winter prior to the first hurling training course in 1965, Ferguson, Nealon and Fr Maher had met to draw up the syllabus for the courses and break down the as-yet undefined skills involved.

'We got the lectures ready in all the different aspects of the skills. We were concentrating very much on skills, not on tactics, competitions or analyses of games – that went on later on.'

As the project evolved, the different skills were illustrated first with still photographs, then with series of photos and finally with a film complete with commentary. In the first year, the course was an immediate success. People came from every county in the country to learn the basics of hurling and the three found themselves swamped with classes that were too large to handle and short of personnel to deal with a fast-evolving situation. It was clear, long before the course started, that what was originally intended to be a one-week programme would have to extend to two weeks.

My dad was one of the students who enrolled on the 1965 course. According to his application form, he wanted to learn about being an instructor himself as well as improving his own game. This was a 35-year-old All-Ireland winning inter-county player nearing retirement from the inter-county scene but he, like many others, was still eager to learn and eager to play. Another student was a man named John Hanley from Clare. These two – both teachers who had already been involved in coaching in their own localities – were approached to help run the extended course for the following year.

From 1966 onwards, the triumvirate had become five and a higher-level 'advance' course was added. This was, Des Ferguson told me in his home in Kells over generous refreshments, in response to the demands of people who attended the course the first year – many of them already considered experts in their field – who were still hungry to learn and to come back and experience the hurling retreat atmosphere of Gormanston.

'So we had to put on an advanced course!' said Des, smiling at how the project blossomed so suddenly. 'Your father, John Hanley and Fr Tommy Maher looked after it.'

Some of the most enthusiastic students were from the weaker counties and from the ones on a tier below the likes of Tipperary, Kilkenny and Cork. 'Galway and Clare were weak at the time and they went big-time into the coaching,' notes Donie, stressing that the Gormanston experience served both counties well in terms of hurling development. Both counties are now classed as strong hurling counties that have won All-Ireland titles in recent decades. Donie attributes their current positions to the coaching courses of Gormanston.

'All-Irelands were won out of those [training camps],' says Diarmuid Healy, 'because they focused in on what hurling was and what coaches should be doing in order to improve their skills and the skills of the players.' Diarmuid Healy is in a position to know this. He comes from Kilkenny – a county which has become in recent years to the world of hurling what the All-Blacks team has become to the world of rugby. He became coach of neighbouring Offaly at a point in time when Kilkenny lorded it in Leinster. Within two seasons, his skills training had the Offaly players cutting out the needless fouling, concentrating instead on playing and controlling the ball and building their confidence in their ability. The result was a senior All-Ireland title in 1981, with a further crown in 1985.

'I was on the Gormanston course of 1969,' Diarmuid told me one evening on the phone from Kilkenny. 'That was the first time I met your father in person and we met several times in Gormanston after that.'

I have only a very vague memory of my father going away to Gormanston some time in the early 1970s. It was a name that I was familiar with – he had mentioned it many times at home, and I remember looking up at him trying to create a picture in my little head as to where or what this Gormanston place was and why he wouldn't be back for a whole week.

One of the principal characteristics that set the Gormanston course apart and made it so effective was, according to Diarmuid, the fact that it was a residential course that went on over a full week.

'It was a secondary-school style set-up. You had the classroom lecture first and then you went out on the field for the practical. That went on for six full days that we were there. It was very well organised with an exam at the end of it. I actually ended up giving those courses later on. I would say that those people revolutionised hurling.'

The revolution was in the manner in which the game of hurling was broken down into a set of individual skills so that the game could then be passed on and taught to other people. By this way, the game of hurling would be promoted and the gospel would be brought to other parts of the country where hurling was not known. The five 'apostles' took on their task with organisation and passion.

'It was they who drew up the syllabus of their own volition and then went to Croke Park with their proposal,' Diarmuid reminds me, making mention also of Croke Park's deep suspicion of this foreign 'coaching' mullarkey. I remember my dad summing up this sort of attitude with a couple of quotations that were related in his usual animated style complete with accurate voice imitation. One was a quotation from a man in a senior position as a Waterford team selector who dismissed the benefits of coaching in saying: 'Look… a fellah either have it or he haven't it. And if he have it, leave him flake away!' Another such quotation was: 'The coach is the thing that you bring the players to the match in.'

I ask Diarmuid about the statement he made in his RTÉ radio discussion on the state of hurling in early 2008 where he said that 'All-Irelands were won from those [Gormanston] courses.' Is he referring to his own All-Ireland successes with Offaly in the 1980s?

'Oh yes. Anything I learned about hurling came from there. It was all based on the Gormanston model of breaking down the skills, showing players how to perform that skill and getting them to practise and practise them.'

In his last coaching assignment, Diarmuid took his own native club Conaghy Shamrocks from junior level to All-Ireland senior club glory in two seasons. 'The Gormanston model was way ahead of (the current weekend coaching initiatives). I often ask Croke Park to revisit those days. The just have, in my opinion, Mickey-Mouse ones, weekend ones only. They just touch on it, but that was an in-depth study of the game; you were immersed in it for a week and everything was done in a very thorough way. It was invaluable.'

Another of the Gormanston graduates was former Cork player and coach of a number of different counties (including Waterford for eight years), Justin McCarthy. Justin was a young 14-year-old, he told me, when he first heard of Ned Power whilst listening to the radio commentary of the inimitable late Micheál Ó hEhir. He played his first senior game for Cork in 1964, by which time my dad was in the twilight of his inter-county career. Justin's senior inter-county hurling career was dogged by injury and his All-Ireland medal haul of just one bears testament to this fact, having been an important part of the Cork senior team when they were doing well.

It was in Gormanston that his and my father's paths crossed. Like Diarmuid Healy, Justin first went to Gormanston in the late 1960s and his first coaching assignment was from 1969 to 1970 when he was unable to play after breaking his leg in a motorbike accident. In true apostolic style, he brought the good news of Gormanston to the enthusiastic but success-starved hurlers of Antrim. Under his tutelage, they won an All-Ireland intermediate hurling title. By 1974, he had returned to his native Cork as a player and was part of their All-Ireland senior victory in 1974. A year later, he was coaching his county to a Munster title before exiting as coach under clouds of controversy and allegations that he was pushed out of the position. After successful stints with Clare (during which they won back-to-back National League and Munster titles), he returned to the Cork county senior scene as joint coach and steered them to All-Ireland victory in the GAA Centenary year of 1984.

Justin notes that '99% of the attendees at Gormanston were teachers.' On the day I spoke to him, we met in a hotel on the outskirts of Cork close to his place of work. As an oil company employee, he was one of the few attending the course that wasn't a teacher – which perhaps explains why he makes a point of mentioning the fact of there being a majority of teachers on the courses. The starting date in early July was partly designed to suit working primary teachers, who would all be on their first weeks of summer leave at that point. In addition, there was the added incentive for teachers of being able to take off time in lieu of the time spent on the course.

'It was very well organised,' Justin remarks, outlining the day's activities of classroom tutorials with hand-outs mixed with practical application, rounded off with a match in the evening. 'We'd also have our own league system and a long-puck competition… There were people from all over the country. It was like going on a retreat for a whole week – a hurling retreat.'

The set-up at Gormanston was, as Justin described, very retreat-like. Located about 40 km north of Dublin, it was a calm, leafy environment sealed off from the outside world and run by the Franciscan monks. There was a mini-golf course and a swimming pool and everyone was accommodated in the dormitories that were normally reserved for boarders.

My father loved going there and always spoke of the place with a wistful shake of the head and a sense of longing. He even once seriously considered sending my brother Seán to boarding school there, even though it was at the other end of the country. He would have loved it because it was a total immersion in hurling. He would have loved the facilities of golf and swimming. He was never a strong swimmer – it was something he never quite got to grips with as a sport – but he loved it for the relaxation it offered. Thirdly, He would have loved it for the retreat-like atmosphere pervaded with a strong ecumenical air that it offered – bringing back many childhood memories of his great days in the CBS in Dungarvan. The Brothers have come in for a lot of stick in recent years – much of it, in my opinion, for very good reason – but my father never had any negative experiences at the hands of the Christian Brothers. It was all encouragement, character-building and positive forces that he experienced and he was very sad to see their rapid demise in Irish society in the last few decades of his life.

In an extract from an article my dad wrote in the *Dungarvan Leader* in 1996, he gives his impressions and memories of the coaching camp:

The Gormanston courses started in 1965 and continued into the late seventies when the GAA bureaucrats decided they had outlived their usefulness. I was there for all of them and will never forget them. Each year seemed to surpass the previous year in enjoyment. Gormanston College is a massive Franciscan second level institution in County Meath some 30 miles north of Dublin. The college possesses every possible educational and recreational facility. Besides dormitories with accommodation for over 300, there is ample provision of private rooms, classrooms, television rooms, language laboratory, a large refectory, a magnificent swimming pool and a beautiful chapel where we occasionally responded to the urge to acknowledge God's munificence to us. The outdoor facilities could hardly be bettered with charming walks through the spacious grounds (we hardly took any notice of them!), several fine playing pitches, a handball alley with covered spectator accommodation, an athletic cinder track to championship standard and a testing nine hole golf course within the confines of the college complex.

The priests were fine men whose broadmindedness, warmth, understanding and hospitality enhanced our stay. They became an integral part of our courses whose spirit and those they shared and they contributed towards making the week an unforgettable experience...

The Gormanston day was long and exhausting. You were very lucky if one of the hurlers didn't rearrange your bedclothes so that it was hard to distinguish it from some kind of maze. Breakfast at 8.30 was followed by the first of the day's talks – I hate the word lecture, it sounds so stuffy and conceited. Then it was out of doors until lunchtime. The weather was invariably bright and sunny – Gormanston is situated in one of the two driest parts of Ireland – so the outdoor skill sessions were always enjoyable and relaxed. Nothing intruded on the even tenor of our ways except the occasional drone of an army plane coming in to land at the nearby airport. How quickly the morning sped by and as lunchtime approached it was customary for one group to challenge its neighbour to a match so that the morning came to a fitting end with a hurling game. The afternoon saw an alternation between the theoretical and the practical and by 4.30, when it was time for the usual match to conclude that session, there were some very tired bodies and aching limbs. What could be more welcome and refreshing than to enjoy the splendid pool before tea.

After tea, there was always some high-profile speaker to entertain us. As both hurling and football courses were run simultaneously we had the opportunity to listen to and question the leading coaches of both games. Kevin Heffernan, famous Dublin player and coach was an entertaining and informative guest and we also enjoyed the views of Mick O'Dwyer, Eugene McGee, Seán Boylan, Fr Michael O'Brien among others. A game of table tennis, handball if you had the energy or a bit of golf took care of the rest of the day. Many elected to pay a visit to the Gormanston Arms or into nearby Balbriggan where the wheels of conversation could be lubricated. It was always late every night when sleep eventually took over.

It was clear that Justin McCarthy thoroughly enjoyed his stay at Gormanston too, from the enthusiastic manner in which he continued to describe the place: 'You'd have eight pitches up there. There was a big influx of people from the North between 1968 and 1972. The Northern lads were great at the sing-songs during the evening.'

Justin describes my father as one who stood out as having a great love for the game of hurling. He was, he says, 'light-hearted' in his dealings with people. 'He had a great style in getting across to people the basics of the game.

'While the game has changed to a large extent, the principles of the game don't ever change. I think that he was very good on the principles of the game, which all coaches have to have but who sometimes forget about them. Sometimes coaches are looking for something else; something more modern. And whilst you can always add on to the principles of the game, keeping the basics is very important and I think that he was a great man for emphasising that.

'Every tennis player or golfer has to have the right stance and hold their club or racket in the right way and when you're a hurler, you're no different because you still have an implement in your hand. Your father also preached time and again the importance of practising those principles over and over. He had a great love for the game coupled with a strong feeling for it too, which allowed him to get it across to other people. You'd tend to feel important that he was telling you something that was certainly the truth and which you would take on board. A lot of people would have a great knowledge of the game but weren't able to get it across to people and your father – perhaps being a teacher – had that great gift of being able to get a message across to people, often in a light-hearted way.'

My dad was never a drinker. He had taken the Pioneer pledge at a young age and kept it going until he was a very mature man – probably about 60. Whilst on holidays in France, my father finally laid his Pioneer pledge to rest. His fondness for France was such that he felt he was missing out on an important aspect of French life by not having a drink of wine. During his Pioneer years, he had always planned to look forward to tasting stout and wine. Try as he did, he found stout completely unpalatable and was truly flabbergasted at the popularity of Guinness. However, he took to enjoying the occasional glass of wine with my mother, provided it was sweet and cheap. In fact, they even managed to horrify my brother who once brought them back a fine bottle of red from his visit to a winery in the *Chateauneuf-du-Pâpe* region, which my parents duly watered down and added sugar to before they would drink it. He also took a shine to cold lager beer. He made sure to get a slab of French beer on the shopping trip to the local *hypermarché*, much to the encouragement of my younger brother Éamonn who, as a teenager at the time, was glad of the opportunity to have the occasional beer with his father.

So I always did wonder how he got on in social situations with a big gang of men, all such occasions seeming to revolve around alcohol consumption in Ireland. I try to picture my dad in these situations and I asked Justin what he was like in the evening when a few drinks and a sing-song would be indulged in.

'He was always very good-humoured, light-hearted… good for a ball-hop too! He was a very good mixer – he could fall into anyone's company very easily. I wouldn't think that he had any real enemies.'

He was a man who concentrated on the minute details which had a bearing on the bigger results, according to Justin, and he took the competitive side of any game very seriously. Yet, at the same time, he never took things completely out of context. I reminded him of our heartbreak at watching a highly fancied Waterford team get beaten by Limerick at the semi-final stage of the All-Ireland competition in 2007. Justin was the Waterford coach for his last full season at that point. At the time of speaking to him, he finds himself, somewhat ironically, in the position of Limerick coach. Waterford had already beaten Limerick in the Munster final that year and all the pundits were expecting Waterford to brush Limerick aside again to meet Kilkenny in the final. I watched the match, along with my older brother Seán, my younger brother Barry and my mother and father. It was only three months before my dad's death but it felt like the shock of a bereavement to us that day, seeing our hopes dashed. I suppose we all felt that this might be the one; that it was destined for Waterford to win another All-Ireland just before my dad died, and the rest of the country seemed to agree with us – except for Limerick, as it turned out. From his bed, however, my father seemed more shocked by how upset we were than by the result itself. As a player and coach, he often reminded us that he lost far more games than he won. He just extended his hand, palm upward, saying: 'It's only a game. That's all it is – just a game.'

Justin nodded when I told him this. For all the fierce rivalry between Waterford and Cork in hurling over the years, here was a dyed-in-the-wool Cork man whose last competitive game as a player was against Waterford and whose first competitive game as a coach was against Waterford, yet who saw no problem in coaching Waterford for seven years, bringing them to many successes of the like that Waterford hadn't seen in over 40 years.

'I was always listening to others for advice along the way about hurling. Of course, with Gormanston, you had the same thing in a much more formalised and organised manner and your dad was certainly one of those who you'd listen to and be influenced by. Sometimes it's the passion of the person or their dedication to the game or their emphasis on small points that would have an impact on you. I'm always learning about the game because the game is so intricate and so varied that you're always trying to pick up ideas of how to put it into play and how to transfer it across and get people to think.

'Possibly, it was a simpler style and people could take things on board because life wasn't as complicated around that time; people would take ideas on board because hurling was very much spoken about more. So, you had people who were mad to learn about it. Today, there are so many other sports to look at, so many other ideas and things to do that sometimes it's harder to get the message across. That time, things were more simple and people had time to listen. Sometimes, I wonder today if people are listening at all.'

The idea of constantly improving was a relatively revolutionary one at that time too. It didn't seem to be in the thinking of the upper tiers of the GAA structure at the time. For my father and others of a similar mind such as Justin McCarthy, this was not the case. Whether as a player or as a coach, you should be always looking to improve and refine. My father was constantly watching people who took a hurley in their hand and correcting their grip or their stance or their swing at every opportunity. Many was the conversation in the staff room of the school in Tallow where my father taught, for example, which was interrupted mid-sentence by my father rushing outside to correct the grip of a child he spotted holding the hurley the wrong way.

My dad's coaching skills weren't ever used to a great extent in the county scene, even though he excelled in Tallow and in every single club that he worked with. The main impediment to him having any strong influence at county level was the very different and politically-charged atmosphere of the county team set-up. A club is simply a group of people who want to see their team do well and is usually composed of passionate people with a common purpose and who are willing to give their time and energy towards making that happen, working with and assisting their coach in whatever way they can.

In the case of a county team, the motivating factors that dictate the behaviour of the people in charge are very different in nature, with the common goal of success for the county being clouded and diluted by personal pursuits of glory and a prevailingly conservative attitude.

Fellow Gormanston graduate and Dungiven-based inter-county coach Liam Hinphy puts it thus: 'I suspect that his unorthodox approach – where he valued the player primarily – would have countered against your father. I know that I experienced the same myself when I ran county football teams and county hurling teams. A lot of county board people devote hours and hours of their time, but it's not terribly constructive. They're terribly jealous of their power and control. A man like your father wouldn't have any part of that, nor would he be wanted, you see. And Ned wouldn't be controlled: he had views of his own and he was steadfast that way.'

My dad was used in the county set-up on just a couple of occasions and only on a peripheral basis. The first was during the 1974 under-21 campaign. Tony Mansfield of Abbeyside – who, as an underage coach, met my father on the field of battle on numerous occasions – was in charge of the team:

'I was managing the under-21 Waterford team,' Tony told me. 'He wasn't a selector, but I brought him in as a coach. I think that he was a man before his time and his greatest forte was never utilised to the extent that they're utilising it now; it wasn't recognised at that time, but we saw it alright… as an individual coach, he could take any player and improve him.'

That under-21 side brought Waterford its very first Munster title when they overcame Clare by 11 points to 6. They went on to the All-Ireland final, where they faced a Kilkenny side. It was an incredibly close match, with the lead changing hands several times in the game before finishing with the narrowest of victories for Kilkenny. The final score was 3-8 to 3-7.

The next experience of involvement in the county team that my dad had was from 1982 to 1983. After close to 20 years of very little happening in the senior Waterford championship campaigns, these were exciting times indeed. Our team had actually made it to a Munster final in 1982. There were even a few Tallow men on the team, including Kieran Ryan, Liam O'Brien and Pat Daly and they were up against Cork. During the 1982 championship, I went to see the matches in Semple Stadium, experiencing for the first time as a 14-year-old the thrill of climbing the concrete steps beneath the stand and emerging into the noisy daylight.

Dad was involved in coaching the team as a sort-of second-in-command to businessman and team manager Joe McGrath. Joe – another Gormanston graduate – was originally from County Down and based in Munster. He was brought in principally for his organisational and motivational skills – something which seemed to come across strongly from the very first time you would meet him. He was friendly with my dad, who was there for his own expert knowledge and All-Ireland experience.

After getting to the Munster final for the first time since 1966, however, I witnessed an unfortunate Waterford team receive a uniquely awful pasting at the hands of an exceptionally good Cork side. The margin was 31 points.

My dad was still there under Joe McGrath the following year, but it was a case of different venue, same result as they went down in their second successive Munster final to Cork – this time by the lesser margin of 19 points.

The Waterford county board decided, thereafter, that they didn't need Joe McGrath as manager any more and my father went with him. His experiences with the county scene then – at a time of ferocious in-fighting and what he saw as a creeping professionalism that went against the grain of what he held important and dear – had left him very disillusioned with it all and not hopeful of any resurgence in Waterford's hurling fortunes for some time to come.

In 1992, however, he was called upon to assist in a very different capacity. The under-21 Waterford team was still being coached by Tony Mansfield and by now also by Peter Power. Peter is from Dungarvan and Tony is from across the one-eyed bridge in Abbeyside. They both knew my father very well and were eager to avail of his expertise but without dragging him into a political set-up for which they knew he would have no stomach.

'Johnny Brenner and Tony Browne were the two fellas who might hit seven good shots and three bad ones – the ball would spin off their hurley,' said Peter to me when I met him in his home in Dungarvan. 'I spoke to Ned about this. We made a video of our next challenge match and I sent it up to Ned. We asked him to watch it and pick out ten faults in the players' techniques. I told him that we didn't want him to pick out anything but faults, because we knew that Ned could see things that we couldn't see.'

My dad sent back the tape a week later with a note attached and ten faults underlined. The main one concerned an occasional habit of midfielder Brenner to twist his hurley ever so slightly as he was about to strike the ball – particularly when taking a free. At the next training session, Peter told his young charge that Ned Power had spotted the reason why some of his shots weren't struck so well. There were also some corrections to be made concerning Tony Browne's outfield striking from his bad side and Paul Flynn's free-taking. Giving advice to young men can sometimes be a delicate balancing act of pride versus humility but advice given by an All-Ireland legend was taken seriously. The players, according to Peter, improved out of all proportions and the team went on to win the All-Ireland under-21 title.

'I don't think people appreciated the knowledge of hurling that Ned had,' said Peter. 'He was able to sum up a player at any age like no-one else could.' In his many coaching positions, Peter would often refer people to my father for extra attention to undo faults or bad habits –

tasks which my dad would willingly take on and always, according to Peter, with excellent results. He noted that the Waterford minor team of 1989 – the bulk of which went on to become the All-Ireland winning under-21 team of 1992 – was an average side that improved unrecognisably over the intervening three years. Much of that improvement, he attributes to the behind-the-scenes advice that he got from my father.

A lot of the time, it was down to simple things, but very often it's the simple things that other people miss. To illustrate the point, Peter tells me about an under-age match where he bumped into my father many years previously. He almost doubled over laughing across the kitchen table as he told me.

They were looking at big goalkeeper who was performing very badly.

'Your man is no good, Ned,' said Peter of the boy who watched yet another ball trickle under his feet.

'Ah now, Peter… Don't be too hard on the boy. It mightn't be his fault.'

'But Ned, he's after leaving in six!'

'Maybe he doesn't know: maybe he doesn't know that he's to stop them. Maybe nobody told him that he's supposed to stop them … '

Another story that Peter had for me about my father coaching children was when he'd be approaching a child about being able to hit the ball from both sides.

'Why don't you try hitting the ball with your other side?' my father would say to the child.

'I can't Sir.'

'You like playing hurling, don't you? It's great fun, isn't it?'

'Yes, Sir.'

'Well, now if you can hit the ball from your left as well as your right, then you'll have twice the fun.'

I referred to the disastrous Munster finals of 1982 and 1983. If he was working with and advising Joe McGrath at that point, how could it have all gone so wrong? But Peter insists that the only time my father got his opinions into a team was 'with us in 1992, and very few people knew that'.

And yet, it just might have gone differently. Around 1960, my father ran for one of three administrative positions on the Waterford Western Board. There were 20 candidates in all, including my dad and James

Tobin. James went on to become county councillor and was from the neighbouring Shamrocks club. There was always a strong but healthy rivalry between Tallow and the Shamrocks and James and my dad were good friends. In the count of first preference votes, my father lost out by just a single vote to James Tobin. Because of the closeness of the two, all of my father's votes were transferred to Tobin, propelling him into the administrative position.

Had he been elected that time, things would have certainly been different. Maybe, like James Tobin, he would have stayed on as an administrator for the next two decades. I don't think so, though. I think that he would soon have grown frustrated and fed up with the politics of it all and would have eventually come back down to grassroots level where he was happiest doing the kind of work that, in his eyes, really mattered.

CHAPTER 18

MY FATHER, THE ARMCHAIR CRITIC

Being the social animal that he was, my father would always tend to engage with the television. If the television said something, then he would have to say something back – generally speaking that is. When it came to sport, he was particularly engaged with what was going on, feeling free to express his opinion on the performance of the team, on the performance of the referee, on the mannerisms, accent or turn of phrase of the commentator, if any of this irritated him.

He had his favourite dramas which held his attention. One was *The Pallisers* – a British period drama from the 1970s which my dad used to love to quote, imitating some of the main characters. I'm still not sure what it was about, but it was one of the rare ones that managed to maintain his interest. Another favourite was *Upstairs, Downstairs* – another BBC drama full of richly drawn characters.

At the other end of the scale was *Top of the Pops*. In the time of my youth, there was very little appearing on the television in the way of pop music, so all my siblings and I would watch TOTP attentively, listening to every act and noting the chart position of every song. All this information carried an immense amount of importance to us – the youth of Ireland of the 1980s – looking to see what was selling and what was not in the British market, and what acts were going to be playing. For a lot of that time, there actually was no Irish chart – no-one was cataloguing and compiling it – something that accentuated the importance of TOTP and the British chart all the more.

In any case, my dad found this serious business of pop music all very amusing and he would often step inside the door when the rest of us were watching the show and offer running commentaries on the performances or the songs. One favourite of his was to calmly note that the lead singer was 'very angry, roaring and shouting into the microphone.' It was fashionable for some singers to adopt a Gothic look, complete with pale make-up, which would prompt my father to suggest that 'that fella probably has worms. He could do with a dose of cod-liver oil or Vivioptal.' Or else, if we were still eating in the kitchen, he might go in to have a quick look at a song and then come back into the kitchen to report that 'there's a fellah inside there and he's beating all around him – pots, pans, everything!' For some reason, it took me a while to work out that he was referring to a drummer when he said this, but I used to find the procedure intensely irritating, as I couldn't sit and watch the bloody thing in peace. At the same time, it was very funny and I can remember almost crying with frustration and yet I couldn't help laughing.

When it came to any sport, he was always keen to watch and even more keen to pass a running commentary on it. If it was hurling, he would be completely engaged in the thing, with his running comments ringing in the air and reverberating from the dining room all round the house. Until such time as poor health and lack of energy dictated otherwise (which was only in his final couple of years), there was only one way that my dad could watch a hurling match, and that was with a passionate engagement with accompanying loud running commentary. Strangely enough, this behaviour was in complete contrast to his normally calm persona on the sideline of an actual match. If truth be told, it would often get so intense that I or one of my younger brothers would feel the urge to vacate the room and retreat to the safety of the kitchen in order to watch the match in less stressful surroundings, or even to simply retreat away from the match altogether and forfeit the pleasure of watching it; a pleasure that was diluted by my dad's incessant ranting/commentary.

His comments consisted of a rich mixture of coaching tips, congratulatory remarks and disdain at poor performance from a player or from the referee: 'Pick it up… pull on the ground… watch it!... He's only got one side… the little touch… Get up, you fool! What's he doing? That fellah is an awful tramp! Stop mouthing off to the referee, you fool! I'm always telling the fellahs below about that! That referee is [counting them out with his fingers] blind, stupid, ugly… blind – did I say that already?'

International rugby matches were a favourite of his too, but he didn't have much time for some of the play of the English and French players in particular ('Look at that dirty animal!... Eughagh!') and he certainly didn't have time for one particular commentator on RTE, who had a habit of understating the level of injury to a player. If an Irish rugby player was lying prone on the turf in a state of extreme agony, having clearly had his eyes gouged in the scrum before being punched, elbowed and kicked by a large French or English brute, Fred Cogley would invariably describe the stricken player as 'looking uncomfortable'. My father couldn't abide this sort of shirking understatement at all: 'Listen to that Cogley fool… Uncomfortable!' he would say, imitating the rather genteel voice of the commentator, whose character seemed to match the gentleman-like image of rugby.

On the more positive side, I remember during the 1978 World Cup that he predicted from an early point that the host side Argentina were going to win the competition because he considered them the most organised and cleanest team in the tournament. His commentary on soccer was usually quieter. Maybe it was out of habit of watching *Match of the Day*. That programme used to be on late on a Saturday night when he couldn't let rip for fear of waking the younger children. From my bed, I would be straining to listen to it, wondering at the absence of paternal running commentary, thinking that perhaps my dad had gone to bed and left the television on. He had no time for the increasing number of 'overpaid idiots' that graced the world of professional football, particularly for the growing legion of those who feigned injury, so I think he became less and less enamoured with the world of soccer, which seemed to be getting filled with characters he didn't like.

With the onset of age and decreasing energy levels, his comments to television became more philosophical than adversarial. About a month before his death, we were watching the Rugby World Cup. Dad was living out his whole day from the confines of the bed at that stage and he had dozed off during the exciting surprise victory for France over the All-Blacks. We had been updating him on how things were progressing with the match, but in his confused state the messages coming through about the sequence of events in the game had become muddled. When my sister arrived later, he said to her: 'Seán said that the French won that match and that some of the All-Blacks were playing for France' (a completely untrue allegation of course, and something inconceivable in the context of international rugby). Still, I think that the notion of fickle loyalties in a professional era struck him as something that had to be accepted and he shrugged and said: 'But, I suppose that's the way it is now.'

CHAPTER 19

TALLOW'S RESURGENCE

Something struck me as I was reading match reports and predictions for the All-Ireland: In 1959, my father was not playing for Tallow, but is listed instead as playing for Dungarvan. Yet, he had been teaching in Tallow for almost ten whole years up to that point.

Wasn't that a little odd? Why had he not shown for Tallow by then? He spent most of his time there and, as a teacher and headmaster of the local school for most of that decade, he had become an integral part of the Tallow landscape, training boys and girls in the basic skills of the game. More importantly, didn't Tallow GAA want a goalkeeper who was part of a successful Waterford senior team?

'Yes, but he wasn't living there until he got his own house,' my mother explained to me, outlining his existence as one of a single man who worked in Tallow, staying in digs in the centre of town and who then cycled or thumbed home every weekend.

When it comes to playing for your county, it's all very straightforward: You simply play for the county that you were born in, or where you would have spent the majority of your life. For instance (although it's far too late for me as I write this), I would play for Waterford as I was brought up there, even though my actual place of birth happens to be the

Bons Secours Hospital in Cork. It's a different matter entirely when it comes to playing for one club or another. You generally play for the club of your town or village of origin. If you move to live somewhere else, then you can play for that if you choose to do so. In fact, it's a perfectly acceptable and a normal state of affairs to do so.

My dad, however, could see no reason why he should change allegiance with the club he played for. Perhaps if he had got married and had a family and a mortgage and was therefore 'settled' in Tallow, then he would have felt that the logical move would have been to play for Tallow. But as a single man, he exercised his choice to remain with his original club.

'He was a bit of a rebel with Tallow when he first came to Tallow because he wouldn't play with Tallow!' said Eddie Cunningham, a friend and lifelong Tallow GAA stalwart who played for and coached Tallow teams. Eddie's involvement with the local club stretches back a long way. He was only 15 when he was made secretary of the club 'because nobody else wanted it….'. Johnnie Curley, another long-time Tallow GAA former player and current selector, told me how he had heard the stories of how Ned Power 'refused' for so long to play for Tallow.

As the years went on, my father's star rose, as his passion for hurling reflected in the constant training that his pupils were receiving and his appearance as a substitute in the 1957 All-Ireland final. But the more Tallow GAA wanted him to play for them, the more my father held his ground in that calm unyielding manner of his. His club was Dungarvan and temporarily Affane and he wasn't going to change his colours now.

By 1959, however, the ante had been upped. He was now a rarity in Waterford – an All-Ireland star. Moreover, he was an All-Ireland star from West Waterford who was working and living in Tallow. Tallow GAA could stand the situation no longer and something had to be done.

In Ireland in 1959, the power of the Catholic Church was as omnipresent and pervasive as the weather itself. As a national school teacher, my father's employer was the state, the Republic for which his father and many others had made sacrifices to establish. But schools were divided (and largely still are) along religious lines. Before the establishment of the republic in Ireland, the Catholic religious were the ones who established and controlled the educational institutions and the emergence of an independent state did not greatly change that state of affairs. The decision-making for Scoil Mhuire NS in Tallow fell to a local board of management, which would have a representation from the Catholic Church on it.

In the case of the main educational institution in Tallow, the practical reality of the situation (and Tallow was certainly not an isolated example of this) was that the board of management consisted of one man – the local parish priest. Even if there was a proper board with other members on it, the truth of the matter is that nobody would go against what the priest would say anyway. So, in a way, the Tallow primary school 'board of management' was a model of efficiency in decision-making. Through a series of intermediaries, the one-man board of Canon Flynn was convinced by Tallow GAA of the urgent need to get Ned Power to play for what had surely become his natural club. Armed with the power of hiring and firing, the parish priest informed my father of this urgent need and my father duly joined Tallow GAA club.

Tallow GAA was well and truly in the doldrums when my father came to town. There had been a successful senior team a decade or so previously. In fact, Tallow had won the county senior title in 1936. By 1950, however, the misery of ration-enforced Ireland was reflected in the decimated state of the Tallow GAA club. The Waterford county GAA scene has always been dominated, to a greater or lesser extent, by the big Waterford city clubs and this was now truer than ever. After years without any sort of success, the club could barely field a junior team.

There was no senior team in 1950 or throughout the 1950s. My father was to be the catalyst to change all that.

One former pupil in Tallow of the era described the arrival of Ned Power to the school as 'like a breath of fresh air.' Here was a young 20-year-old teacher who brought with him a totally fresh approach to the whole business of teaching. He was energetic and entertaining and, as with any task he undertook (whether playing Gaelic football, hurling, tennis, cycling back to Dungarvan at weekends), he applied himself to it with as much zeal as he could.

A significant development in those early years in Tallow was that my father became principal in what you would have to say was an abnormally short space of time. The system in primary schools in Ireland is that, all things being equal, he or she who is the longest-serving teacher gets to be the principal of the school. At the time of my father's arrival, there were two primary schools in Tallow itself. Divided along the lines of gender, my Dad was in the boys' school, which was located opposite the Catholic Church on Chapel Street. There were just two other teachers in the boys' school along with my dad – Mr O'Leary and his wife.

While primary teaching is a career that gives as much security as a job could offer, the flip-side of it – and one which many find difficult to deal with – is that promotional opportunities are limited and often very hard to come by. Most teachers go through their entire lifetime as teachers without becoming principal, but my Dad, through a series of fortuitous events (for him, at least), had been fast-tracked to principal-ship in a time-frame where most teachers would be only finding their feet and was to be the head teacher in Tallow before the decade was out.

From the word go, he started to instil a love of hurling into the hearts and minds of the youth of Tallow. It was hurling country anyway, so he was certainly not preaching a new religion to people in West Waterford. The generation that he was dealing with, however, had known only failure to be the lot of the Tallow GAA in terms of performance on the field – a generation believing that they were inferior to other clubs in the county.

Tallow GAA did not have any field of its own at that time. Moreover, there was no money around for many children to be able to afford the basics of a hurley and a ball.

'Your father used to train in Aquin Murphy's field,' Eddie Cunningham told me. There was also a field known as Curley's field, which was used on and off by the local club as disputes erupted and became resolved and then erupted again. 'When you think of it now… We used two coats for the goals. Your father would go in goals and I'd be taking shots at him. We practised up there; we practised in Keefe's field behind the graveyard of the Church – he was allowed in there; Mort Kelleher allowed him into the Bride Valley field alongside the graveyard; we hurled in the big Barracks field. Just the two of us – I was only a young fella at the time – and there was nowhere else to train.'

Facilities did not, of course, include such luxuries as a changing room. It was a case of togging off by the ditch at the side of the field. With Curley's field, there were stables and if the horse wasn't there, then you could tog off in the relative comfort of the stable.

'I always said he [Ned] was a man before his time where coaching was concerned,' says Eddie Cunningham.

'There's no doubt about that,' says Johnny Curley. He was born around the time that my father first came to Tallow and was one of the first generation to grow up under the direct influence of my father as a teacher and a hurling coach – two roles that blended seamlessly into one in reality. 'The schools thing was something that came across big time, because he was always ball-and-hurley. Ground hurling was his first love; catching the hurley the right way. In fact, some fella could be very good and still catching the hurley the wrong way, but your father would be there saying: "You can't hurl like that, you're catching the hurley the wrong way!" '

By the early 1960s, my dad was firmly established as a Tallow player and a star of one of the best inter-county senior hurling teams in the country. Moreover, as a teacher and a member of the GAA club, his presence was beginning to be felt in the beginnings of what was to become a series of skilful Tallow hurling sides.

Tallow GAA club's history goes back to the very early days of the GAA itself. There was certainly a GAA club in Tallow by 1887 and it's possible that there was one there earlier than that. In the beginning, the club had only a football team, but in 1919 a hurling club was established and it was hurling that was to be the dominant sport.

They won a senior county hurling title in 1936, but thereafter the club's fortunes slipped and by the time my father arrived, there was no senior team. So, things had to start from scratch for Tallow GAA. The first signs of a life reborn came in 1962 when Scoil Mhuire NS won the Avonmore League. This was an underage GAA league competition in West Waterford that was sponsored by the dairy food company Avonmore (now absorbed into the much larger company Glanbia, who sponsor both the Kilkenny and the Waterford senior hurling teams). Two years later, it was the turn of the hurlers, who became champions in the same competition.

This was to be no fluke result. Through the direct influence of my father, Tallow was producing a whole new generation of skilful hurlers and footballers that were to take title after title at almost every single level. Tallow GAA club existed long before my father was even born and its resurgence from the early 1960s onwards was not the sole result of just one man: He became part of the set-up that involved a number of dedicated people.

From every single person I have spoken to, however, comes the story that it was my father who was the single most important influence on that resurgence and it was he who effectively coached entire generations of Tallow youths who went on to become skilful senior players that allowed Tallow to compete at the highest level in hurling.

'It [the Avonmore League] was the seed for Tallow of what came on afterwards,' says Billy Sheehan. Billy's family is steeped in Tallow GAA tradition and he is a former pupil of my father's, as well as having taught in Naomh Mhuire himself, where he became principal and he played for Tallow at senior level. 'At the time in Tallow, there was no permanent hurling field there. We used to go out to Curley's field for training – that's where all those schools league matches were played. The Avonmore League was also important because you had adult teams and minor teams but you didn't have anything below that until those leagues started in the early 1960s.'

In the mid-1960s, the under-16 competitions came into being and the official GAA under-14 competitions started at the end of the decade.

'The 1960s and 1970s were like a rollercoaster ride,' continues Billy, before clarifying that 'although there were some disappointments, it was generally a case of the grass growing up and up. From a GAA point of view, what was a big thing was buying a field. They bought the field in 1963 and then they had a permanent home. As far as I know, although the deal was done then, it wasn't paid off until the mid-1970s. I remember Ned being in great form one day at school and saying that "we finally paid off the field" '.

'You had other people involved [in Tallow GAA], but Ned was coming from the school, so all the lads who had trained and played with them had come through the school with him. And, once they started up these Avonmore Leagues and they continued year after year, he was in charge of those teams – 3rd class, 4th class, training them three times a week.'

It must also be noted that the footballing origins of Tallow GAA were confined to folklore at this point and the club didn't even have an actual football when they were playing their first games in the Avonmore Leagues. So, although a hurling man first and foremost, my father played a major part in reviving Tallow's lost footballing tradition too.

Tallow's next important landmark was again in football, when the under-16 team beat Mount Sion to win a county title in 1966, of which Billy was the captain: 'The unusual thing about that match is that it was played in Carrick-on-Suir. So you had a Waterford county final played in County Tipperary, which is most unusual. But the reason was that Ned was playing in goals for Waterford and they were playing Tipperary in a league match. Seamus Power was also playing with the Waterford hurling team and he was involved in the Mount Sion under-16s, so to accommodate the two of them, the county final was played in another county… That was a massive win. After that, county finals started coming.'

Compared to the barren decades that had gone before this time, there was a virtual avalanche of titles, as Tallow won county honours at every level, with the sole exception of a senior football title. Just why my dad made all the difference was explained to me by Billy: 'First of all, every child that played with Tallow had gone to school with Ned. So every child had been taught the skills in exactly the same way. Secondly, Ned had a vision of the way that Tallow should hurl, so everybody that played with Tallow knew that vision and that style of hurling. And the fact that Ned was involved from the very lowest level constantly coaching meant that Tallow continued with that style for the next 20 years as far as I'm concerned and Tallow had a very distinctive style of hurling, which goes back to the schools and it goes back to Ned and his work at schools level. Every fella knew what was expected of him, no matter what position he was played in.

'For example, the current Kilkenny team have a very distinctive style but every Kilkenny team is playing the same way – they have the same style of hurling. That was us back then. We had our own style of hurling which suited us and everybody bought into it. I wouldn't say that nobody else was doing it, but we were better because we were tactically aware of what we were about… we were better coached and we had better skills. Even to this day, Tallow teams are very skilful teams. That's Ned's legacy as far as I can see.'

In getting the best out of players of all levels, my dad would always encourage and accentuate the positive. Former pupil, underage player and senior county hurler Pat Daly remembers:

'It was never a case of Tallow weren't good enough – they were always better. That was the line he always adopted… I wouldn't have been big into pep talks, but my abiding memory is when we were playing in Cappoquin one time in what must have been an under-10 match. Your father had always been onto me to kick from my left leg. I was dodgy enough on it, but on this night, I decided that I'd better kick from my left leg. So I did and it went straight out over the sideline.

'The following day, he came around with the roll book into my class room. I was thinking: I hope he doesn't mention the match, and he did. Then I thought: I hope he doesn't mention my name, and he did! He said: "Where's Pat Daly?" He called me up and he said: 'I want to congratulate you because you did what I always wanted you to do; you kicked with your left leg. Now it didn't work out with you last night but it will work out." '

Eddie Cunningham also remembers the dramatic influence that my father had over the years on Tallow GAA's fortunes, and, by extension, on the psychological well-being of the town: 'Buying the field was the big thing, because then your father could take the young fellas down training after school. And he was a hero to them because he had won an All-Ireland medal by then, so they listened to him.'

From 1966 onwards, Eddie recalls that the under-16s football title was a major milestone. Under-16 level was only a few short years away from senior level and this was a proper, official GAA level too. The Avonmore League was a great starting point because the GAA didn't have competitions in Waterford at that level, but now Tallow could hold their heads high and say that they were the best in the county at football at the officially recognised under-16 level. And everyone in Tallow GAA were only too well aware that this was simply the beginning; that those under-16s would be playing senior in a matter of years; that behind them would come an even bigger number of players, all trained in the Ned Power mould, coming off the conveyor belt of a production line.

All of this was coinciding nicely with an economic resurgence in the country in general. Under Seán Lemass (who served as Taoiseach from 1959 to 1966), Ireland was beginning to resemble the kind of modern permissive society that the rest of Europe, broadly speaking, had already become. It was the showbands era – where the big regular social events were concerts given by Dickie Rock or the Dixies in the local dance hall. But they were still times of relative poverty compared to now – material possessions of the average household would have been meagre enough and there were still few enough who had a car that would be able to transport players on an increasingly busy match-playing programme. Christy Walsh's truck was typically full of players.

'Sonny O'Brien used have a car,' says Eddie Cunningham about the late former treasurer of the club, who was a car-dealer. 'Your father had a car… we used to use Jim Collins' van if we were stuck. But ye were all at home of a summer's Sunday often while he was gone off with the car. He would often say it to me how he felt guilty about bringing a load of fellas off to a match instead of bringing all of ye to the seaside.'

My dad's guilt about being somewhere else instead of at home is something that he must have had all through his life as a husband and father. I never spoke to him about it, but the fact is he was devoted to the GAA – very much so. As a consequence, his GAA activities took him away from the family. It certainly must have rankled with my mother. I'm also sure that it rankled with my older siblings. As for me, I think that the intensity of his GAA activities had reached their peak before I was a conscious being, so although he may have been out of the house on GAA activities, I didn't feel that he was missing from the home so much as doing important work that needed to be done. If I had a gripe with him, it would be the demands that everyone else seemed to make on him – stopping him on the street to get a few words with him, not only in Tallow, but absolutely everywhere that we went. No place was safe. Even on the beach in Les Sables d'Olonne – 1,000 km from home – Pat Hartigan of Limerick saw him and came over to talk to him.

Frank Fitzgerald and Willie Brien were another two that were among the few that provided transport on a regular basis for Tallow's sporting warriors. 'Willie O'Brien had a Volkswagen (Beetle). He could have ten young fellas inside in the car.'

The bandwagon was well and truly rolling now. By this stage, everyone (not just my father) could see where it was going and on it rolled, collecting silverware along the way. Tallow's first under-16 hurling county title duly arrived in 1967, when they also won a minor title. In 1972, it was the turn of the under-21 team and then, in 1974 came the breakthrough intermediate county title. This was a momentous landmark win because this meant that Tallow were now in the big boys' league of senior hurling. They even had a few players on the Waterford under-21 side that had reached the All-Ireland final.

In an interview given in the early 1990s, my father was asked to highlight some of his greatest moments and achievements as a player. In typical fashion, he refused to single out any of his achievements because, he said: 'quite honestly, I think – as I've always thought – the team is more important than one player and the place is more important than any one team, but I will say this much: To me, it was a great fulfilment when Tallow won the intermediate championship in 1974, which made Tallow a senior team again. That was the culmination of all our strivings.'

'That was a great year,' remembers Johnny Curley of that breakthrough year. 'It was the first year that I could get on a team and stay on it! We went to Red Barn that night celebrating... It was a great thing for the town. It was the first big win and for ten years or more after that, we were winning every second year.'

My father was also playing on that team, as was Billy Sheehan: 'That night in 1974 was a huge thing for Ned because he had taken these youngfellas up the ranks and brought them to senior level, where he thought they belonged. For the older generation like Pa Sheehan, Noel

Condon and Harry Ronan, it was a huge thing for them seeing Tallow back up playing senior. I remember that night there were fellas out in the pubs that I had never seen out in my life. And it wasn't that they were out drinking, but they were so happy to share in the joy of the moment.'

But playing in the big boys' league presented its own challenges. They were now, as Billy Sheehan remembers, 'up against the Ballygunners and the Mount Sions. In our minds, they were up there and we were down here. So it was Ned's job to make us believe that we were up as high as them or above them. That was a huge task. It's like asking a team today to get it into their heads that they can beat Kilkenny in hurling or Kerry in football. That was a huge thing that he had to do and I think that that was one of the biggest things that he succeeded in doing; to get fellas to believe that you're playing, say Mount Sion in Dungarvan and you can beat them – you can beat them if it's wet, you can beat them if it's dry and you can beat them if it's a Sunday night.'

As the titles mounted, so the confidence grew. Billy himself remembers as a youth feeling some of that growing confidence in Tallow's general ability to take on the world and beat them in one incident where a member of the minor football team was asked if they thought they would win. The reply was: 'Of course we'll win… sure, we're Tallow!'

Tallow's first shot at a senior county title came in 1976 – in their second year of the senior championship. Perhaps the job of making them believe that they were better than their opposite numbers wasn't done yet or perhaps they simply weren't yet good enough. Whatever the reason, they were given a sobering lesson in the fortunes of sport when they were thrashed by a margin of 23 points by Portlaw. Playing on the opposing side was my dad's former Waterford team-mate and much-admired friend Tom Cheasty. This was a major blow to Tallow's confidence. After having made relatively unhindered and steady progress through the other levels, they were stopped dead in their tracks in a most humiliating way and it was to be another four years before they would be in a county final again.

'It was a big setback,' remembers John McDonnell, who was on the team. 'We were at an age where the nucleus of the team was 26, so we should have been winning and one of the reasons I think we lost is because we were over-confident. And when that begins to fall back on you, it's like a domino effect.'

But they were back in a county final in 1980. Under manager Eddie Cunningham, and with my father installed as coach, they took on

Dunhill – the favourites who were going for three in a row – and beat them by a single point on a score line of 1-7 to 1-6. The first senior title in 44 years for the club was greeted with great scenes of jubilation. I was 12 at the time and have strong memories of the whole place going wild, with the team being paraded around the square on the back of a lorry at night and lots of speeches being given. Having grown up in a household so immersed in the day-to-day of hurling and having grown up in a Tallow that was accustomed to regular hurling success, I believed Tallow to already be the best team in Ireland, so it actually came as a bit of a shock to me to see what a big deal this victory was. That's overconfidence.

But it was a big deal in every sense of the word, and the senior county title was complemented by a county title from the minor team one week later, a team on which my brother Seán was playing. The next target was the Munster club title and, thereafter, the All-Ireland club title. They didn't get past the next match, however, which was against Roscrea of Tipperary, but in February of 1981, there was to be bad news of an altogether more serious variety.

Raymond O'Brien – affectionately known as 'Pigeon' – was one of the skilful stars of that senior Tallow team and he was also a rising star on the Waterford senior team, although he was still only 19. He had what my dad called the 'wristy swing' – a delicate but deadly accurate way of stroking the ball with maximum power and efficiency, as well as being an all-round excellent player with a mastery of hurling skills. He was of relatively slight build, which is to say that he wasn't a powerful bulk of a man that could bash through walls, but instead was all speed, skill and efficiency. In other words, he was the sort of player that epitomised what hurling was all about in my father's eyes: Hurling was a sport of skills that needed to be coached, practised and mastered. A team of skilful hurlers was capable of beating anyone – a lesson that the likes of the Kilkenny county teams at all levels take to heart. While he was a patient at the North Infirmary Hospital in Cork, he fell from a 2nd-floor window and died as a result of his injuries in an ambulance on its way to Cork Regional Hospital on the 27th of February in 1981.

The Tallow club was, by now, also producing players of exceptional talent that made the Waterford county team, such as Kieran Ryan, Pat Daly and Liam O'Brien. One of the most talented of all of them was a player called Séamus Treacy. He took on the nickname 'Trasher' as a play on the Gaelic version of his surname (Ó Treasa). When I visited my father in hospital in late 2006, he spoke of him with immense fondness and with a strong sense of a flawed genius who should have gone on to be hailed by the whole nation as one of the greatest hurlers. He, in common with the late Ray O'Brien, was of a light build, making up for what he lacked in bulk or stature with an innately fine-tuned series of skills that left most others for dead. But, unlike 'Pigeon', he had a persistent struggle with alcohol. He was like the George Best of Tallow hurling. If he turned up on the day of a match, he would typically be operating at perhaps 50% of his capacity, one former team-mate told me. But even at that, he could run rings around any opponent with lightning speed. 'He was one of the greats. He truly was.' my father said forlornly that evening, shaking his head. I think that he saw Séamus as someone who had a special talent and he possibly felt it as something of a failing on his own part that he wasn't able to help him to achieve redemption through his talent, through hurling and through the team.

By the time of Tallow's next progression to a county final in 1984, Dad had been called upon to assist other teams who were looking for some of the Midas Touch of Ned Power and wasn't involved directly in the Tallow senior team.

'It was Eddie Cunningham who was doing most of the training,' recalls John McDonnell, 'and Ned was called in to "polish us off" for the final.'

In preparing the team for the match, my father invited a senior team from Blackrock in Cork to come and play them. Blackrock is an illustrious club from a county that has enjoyed a lot more success than Waterford. The practice game was to serve to show the Tallow team that they were at the level of the likes of Blackrock if they would simply play with belief. There were also some key improvements made in the interim, but the victorious result for Tallow was a major boost to their confidence.

But friendlies and warm-ups count for little when the reality of a big championship match dawns. Tallow's opponents were Portlaw – the team that had so humiliated them eight years previously in another county final. This time, Tallow were rank outsiders and the betting odds were tipped at four-to-one. My dad used this fact to his advantage in the pre-match team talk in the dressing room. He spoke to the team about what the local papers were saying, about what people were saying in Tallow, in Portlaw and elsewhere about their expectations for the Tallow team and, of course, about the betting odds of four to one.

'Four to one?' he asked, his face full of incredulity. 'Do you know what that means? That means that each one of their players is four times better than each one of our players.' He turned to the first player:

'So, Liam… that means that your opposite number is four times better than you. Do you think he is?'

'No!'

'And what about you, Frankie? Is your opposite number four times that man that you are, with four times as much skill? Sure, if that's the case, what are we doing here? We might as well get togged off again and go home. But of course we don't believe that, do we?'

By the time he was finished his pep talk, the team was literally bursting to get out the door and onto the field. The game was over as a contest long before the half-time whistle and Tallow were senior county champions again, winning comfortably and upending the bookmakers' predictions by finishing comfortable winners on a scoreline of 2-12 to 2-1.

The following year, my dad was still with the senior team when they recorded their second county title in a row, beating local rivals Ballyduff in the final by one goal. In their next match, they played against the Tipperary champions Kilruane McDonaghs in the Munster club semi-final. Tallow only lost by the narrowest of margins after a scintillating game against the team that was to go on to become All-Ireland club champions that year.

Having reached such heights of achievement, Tallow's fall from grace was to be swift the following year. They were so poor in the next season that they were back playing intermediate level. It must have been a great disappointment to them all that they weren't able to build on their successes. But psychological motivation is funny thing. In the case of Tallow, they were motivated to win the county championship and to give the countrywide club competition a fair go. Having won the county title two years running, perhaps they had no more to prove. They had had a go at the club championship and, although they didn't win anything there, they had proven that they were as good a side as the All-Ireland champions in their one-point semi-final defeat to the eventual winners. This, perhaps, left them with a sense of nothing left to prove to anyone and it was proving to people that they were a good side that was such an important part of the motivational process that got them their back-to-back titles in 1984 and 1985.

Another important factor is fatigue. As one former player pointed out, he was listening to my father talking to him since he was 11 years old until he was 39. The best of motivators and the best of coaches can say the same thing in only so many ways. The other aspect to this phenomenon is that my father was a perfectionist and perfection was something he was continually striving towards. You would not see him jumping up and down with joy on the sideline and he was never entirely happy at a match. The very nature of getting players to improve the different aspects of their game unavoidably involves them being given out to on a regular basis. Not that my father was one to shout and gnash the teeth too much, but listening to the same person giving out to you has a finite lifespan.

Tallow did bounce back to the senior ranks in 1987, but they haven't won a senior county title since, although there is still a strong legacy of skilful players there; the senior team got to the semi-final in 2008 and the under-21 side won county titles in 2002 and 2003.

After Dad died, my sister Patricia received a letter from someone in the neighbouring town of Cappoquin. Growing up in West Waterford, he was very familiar with Tallow teams of the 1970s and 1980s and my father's role in their performance and development. Like many neighbouring towns, they looked on at Tallow's progression with a certain amount of envy but with an element of respect too. His letter, reproduced here with his permission, expresses very eloquently the view from the sideline, as it were.

Dear Tricia,

Please find enclosed a belated Mass card for Ned. As I mentioned to you at the funeral, I have very fond memories of the man, from roughly the age of 12 onwards, doing battle with Tallow teams for a very long time. I can recall the excitement I felt when, after Cappoquin playing against Tallow in an under-14 match, your father and my father arranged it so that my dad would pick up Mick Geary and myself from school in the Friary and Ned brought us back. It was great to be chauffeured at age 13 by an All-Ireland winner. Of course, your dad's commitment to the cause was also shown by the fact that, after he had dropped Mick and myself at the Friary, he went on to De La Salle in Waterford with Con Ryan after that.

When we played against Tallow, there were always two things guaranteed. One was that, no matter who you were marking, he would always be able to hurl and the second certainty was that he

1984 Champions
The Tallow senior team that won the Waterford county title against Portlaw, 1984.

1985 Champions

The Tallow senior team that won the country title against Ballyduff, completing a 2-in-a-row in 1985.

Opening of the School, 1982

The Bishop of Waterford shakes hands with a pupils' guard of honour for the opening of the new primary school in Tallow in 1982. Dad is on the left. The author is second from right.

Schools Team

An under-14 selection from 1984. My brother Éamonn is at the back in the middle wearing a black helmet.

Power Boys
Dad (far right) & his brothers (L to R) Seán, Brendan and Pat at Pat's book launch, Clonmel 1990.

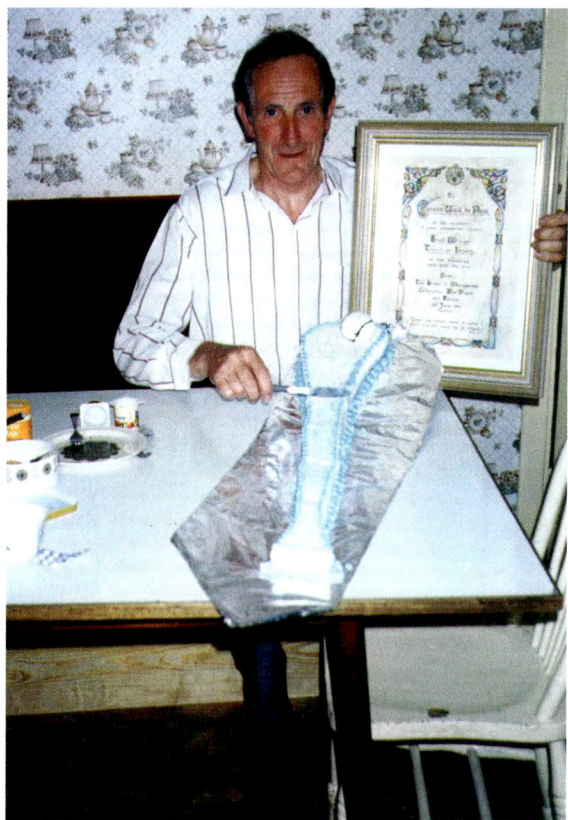

Yum yum!
*A retired principal about to tuck
into a cake in the shape of a hurley
and ball, 1990.*

Power Home
The family home in Tallow, circa 1994.

Reading in the Sun
My dad reading in sunshine, on holiday in Jersey, circa 1998.

Co. Waterford
Minor Champions 1997

Minor Champions

The Tallow minor hurling team that won the county title in 1997. My brother Barry is the goalkeeper in yellow at the back.

Bertie the Gooseberry
Taoiseach Bertie Aherne poses between my parents at the WLR sports awards, Dungarvan 2002.

The Three James Bonds
*My three brothers (L ro R) Barry, Seán and Éamonn do their best secret agent poses at the
WLR sports awards, Dungarvan 2002.*

Déise Heroes Past and Present
Dad poses with 1959 team-mate Tom Cheasty (centre) and Waterford All-Star Ken McGrath (right), December 2004.

Waterford Man in Venice
Dad & Mam relaxing in a gondola in 2002.

Big Night in Croke Park
A rare photo of the entire family in Croke Park on April 1st, 2006, on the occasion of Dad being awarded a President's Award.

would never pull a dirty stroke. I give your father huge credit for this. There were a lot of other teams around the place, Cappoquin included, who would occasionally do the dirt a bit in order to win. My memories of Tallow are actually the opposite. Their hard men, like Johnny McDonnell and Billy Sheehan, were as clean as they came, while the likes of Thrasher and the Curleys had more skill, learnt from the maestro himself, than we could ever dream of. It is no joke, but I can actually remember on two occasions being hit by Tallow guys during senior matches, more or less accidentally, and on both occasions they immediately asked if I was OK (Connie Curley and Liam Moroney). That stuff was bred into them on the hurling fields by Ned.

I was always struck by the fact that a lot of team mentors were almost always very loud, shouting at us, the referee, occasionally at the opposition, etc. Ned, by contrast, had the sort of voice that managed to carry all across the pitch but still seemed to just be talking. The most aggressive thing I remember him shouting was actually 'Bang!' simply to encourage a bit of pulling. What was always unusual was that, on the odd occasions when one of our lads might have done something spectacular, you could hear Ned quietly saying something like: 'That's a lovely stroke', etc. We didn't go in for that kind of magnanimity, I'm afraid.

I have a memory of playing for the Waterford minors in 1977 or '78, against Kerry somewhere in Limerick. Eddie Cunningham was one of the selectors and he asked Ned to come along to give us a short talk on the pitch before the game. As we huddled around, Ned began speaking about the Déise, glory days, crisp hurling, etc. Next thing, out came the Kerry team, running close by us, and Ned stopped in mid sentence. We were all wondering what was going on as he just looked around at the Kerry lads and seemed to be counting 'one, two, three… six!' He then turned back to us and said, very simply: 'Six new hurleys! Imagine turning up to play Waterford in the Munster championship with 40% of the team having to be given a hurley before the match. Go out and show them what Waterford are made of, and that we don't take kindly to teams coming along as if they are going for a walk in the park against us.'

Cappoquin and Tallow played each other in four under-21 finals in a row between 1978 and '81. I was fortunate to have been the captain in 1980, when we won a titanic struggle by something like 4-5 to 2-9. The sort of sportsmanship which Ned fostered was epitomised by the fact that not only did Tallow stay around for the presentation, and for the few words I said in accepting the cup, but Frankie Ryan, captain of Tallow, also made a short speech of congratulations to Cappoquin on the win. I have still never since seen a losing captain make a speech at the end of a final like that. Again, you can bet it was the sort of thing Ned would have encouraged. I am almost certain that he was also the writer of an account in the Tallow notes the following week about the match. It still makes the hairs stand on my neck when I read it, such was the clear love of hurling and of good sportsmanship that came through in the report.

My last time meeting Ned was a couple of years ago. He was on the sideline at an under-age football match in Cappoquin. I walked past on my way down to the lower pitch, where we had a camogie training session going on. As we said hello, it dawned on me to go back and ask him would he call down to give the girls a few encouraging words if he got a chance after the game he was watching. He duly did so. His pep talk to the girls was vintage Ned, all about skill, speed and doing what your trainers told you to do. For the whole five minutes, he was swinging the hurley as if it was part of him. It was worth a fortnight of training to us, no question.

Anyway, Tricia, I won't bore you with any more hurling stuff. I have always had the greatest of respect for Tallow since my under age hurling days. I like to think I still have a lot of friends there, which I put down to the spirit Ned imbued his teams with. You basically worked and worked on your skill, played the game hard and fair and congratulated your opponent afterwards. I think it was a marvellous thing that the club did in naming the field after him before he died. It was an honour richly deserved. He was a true gentleman and I know a lot of people here in Cappoquin were greatly saddened by his passing.

Look after yourselves, OK.

CHAPTER 20

MY FATHER, THE GAELGÓIR

My dad had a passion for the Irish language. He spoke it and wrote it with a fluency that was as easy and natural as his mother tongue of English. Growing up in what was very much a Republican household did have an influence on my dad's love of his country and of his native culture and language. His father would have been on the Republican side in the Civil War, although thankfully he didn't find himself directly involved in the killing that was part of that conflict. But my dad's love of Irish would have come from him in the first place as the serious patriarch that my grandfather apparently would be prone to using Irish in the home on occasion, reserving the Gaelic to describe certain things exclusively. This love of Irish is evident not only in my father's use of the Gaelic tongue but also in that of his brothers. Afterwards, his education at the Christian Brothers reinforced this strong nationalist attitude. At CBS Dungarvan, under the tutelage of such teachers as Brother Murray, the importance of all the cultural aspects of the fledgling Republic were writ even more clearly to him.

Through Gaelic games and the Irish language, a unique voice was created for the expression of Irish nationalism. These were things that were uniquely Irish; which no-one else in the world had; which were as foreign to the British as anything they would have come across in the lands they had subjugated around the globe. It was this sense of creating something entirely different to England that gave Ireland some sort of separate national identity. Any time I was in France – and particularly during my time in college there – I'd often find myself in a political debate trying to explain to people that no I'm not from the 'British Isles' (or les *Îles britanniques*) and yes, it is a completely different country with its own culture and currency and independence. But, viewed from afar, the collection of islands we live on has a long shared history, language and culture. So it's with a sense of almost desperation that we hang on to anything that will separate us from our near neighbours and historical tormentors.

This strong sense of nationalism that has passed on, almost unwittingly, to myself and my siblings owes a lot to the strength of nationalism of my father. Many people I've come across since in life have marked me down as a bit of a Sinn Féin supporter – something of an extremist. It's true that during the polarising times of the 1980s while conflict was ongoing in Northern Ireland, political views like mine tended to be muted. But as far as I was concerned, I was simply giving expression to a simple idea of nationalism and participating in my own small way towards the cultural definition of Ireland.

I think that my father thought like this. He was all for precision and clarity in all things in life and when he approached something or did something, anything, he did it thoroughly and tried not to leave any ill-defined grey lines when he did it. We had a revolution and we had a Republic and I think that he looked upon it as his duty and the duty of every Irish citizen to cultivate the identity of what was after all a new nation, wherever possible.

The sport and the language of Ireland were two important elements of this expression. From an early age, he used the Irish form of his name wherever possible – Éamonn de Paor. Our family name is a Norman one and you can see the French influence in the original Gaelic version of it more easily than the glossed-over anglicised version of Power. It was something I didn't quite appreciate as a little boy, when I'd take the post from the postman in the morning and wonder at why my father used to get letters using some sort of coded version of his name. 'What does that say?' I remember asking my mother.

'That's your father's name.'
'That says Éamonn. I thought he was Ned.'

'He is. That's his real name – his name in Irish.'

'Why is it in Irish?'

'Because he's Irish. We're Irish.'

I gave up asking questions at that point but it took me a number of years before that explanation made any sense to me. In a way, it still doesn't and even though I think it's important to keep the language alive, the impracticalities of using the Irish version of my name seem a bit too much for me. But he wasn't alone in his family in using the Irish version of his name. Both his brother Seán and Brendan are both prone to using their Irish names. His late brother Dr Patrick C Power would also sometimes use the Irish version and he too was a strong Irish scholar. In fact, it was my uncle Pat who translated Brian O'Nolan's classic comic novel *The Poor Mouth* into English from the original Gaelic version.

During the course of everyday life, Dad would use Irish whenever he could. He did have a *fáinne nua* which, for some reason, he had stopped wearing by the time I realised what it was. I had found out from an advertising campaign on television that people who spoke Irish could speak to other people who spoke Irish and they could all recognise one another by the wearing of the smart-looking ring. I said to my father that he should wear one, and he then showed me the one that he had all along but, for reasons known only to himself, he didn't wear any more.

Maybe he didn't like the labelling of it – maybe it attracted unwanted conversation from other people that he didn't want to converse with in any language. Or maybe he didn't want people looking at him like he looked like he was some part of an elite club. That's something that would certainly not have appealed to a man with such a strong socialist heart as my dad had.

So my father continued to practise and promote the Irish language in his own way. He was a great supporter of the now-defunct *Irish Press* for its nationalist agenda as well as for the generous piece of Irish that it had. In latter years, he came round to taking the *Irish Times* on a regular basis and it continues to have a regular column in Irish.

With certain people, he would communicate only in Irish and it always felt a bit strange when he would go through a whole conversation in Gaeilge with someone, who would then turn around and speak to us in his perfect English.

When I asked Billy Sheehan – former principal at Tallow's Naomh Mhuire primary school and former pupil of my father and a former

Tallow hurler – what was his outstanding memory of my dad as a teacher, he said it was his love of Irish:

'The Irish would be one thing that would stand out for me. He was terrific at the Irish. He had a great interest in it and he was a great speaker. Even when he retired as a teacher, he'd keep listening to Irish programmes and read the papers in Irish.'

John McDonnell was another former pupil of my dad and was, in his day, a star hurler with the Tallow senior team. In common with a number of other Tallow boys at the time, he went to De la Salle boarding school in Waterford city. The Tallow contingent in the prestigious college stood out well, but particularly when it came to Irish, as John remembers: 'There'd have been fellas like John O'Brien, Denis McDonnell, George McDonnell, myself and Paul Ryan. Every one of them were probably the best in their class at Irish, because of Ned Power. He was an exceptional Irish teacher altogether.'

After retirement, he would never refuse to help out anyone who wanted to improve their Irish, whether they were adults or children studying for their Leaving Certificate. Rather like the hurling, he was delighted to be able to spread the gospel as far as it would go.

One of his most effective and significant uses of Irish came in the early 1970s. He was attending a Waterford county board meeting to discuss the issue of Rule 42 – the rule that banned GAA members from playing 'foreign' field sports.

My father had always considered this rule ridiculous. Not only had he suffered himself as a result of the rule in the 1950s, but friends of his had also. For instance, Tom Cheasty had been banned when he was spotted at a local dance that had been a fundraiser for a soccer club.

That particular meeting went on until very late in the evening as the debate raged on the issue. For his part, my father opted to make a speech in Irish. He played on the phonetic similarity between the English word 'ban' and the Irish word 'bean' meaning wife or woman.

'Níl ach "bean" amháin agamsa,'* he told the assembled audience.

The paradox of it was that the majority of upholders of the ban, these stalwarts of Irish culture and identity, had, for all their efforts in defence of us in the face of foreign influence, not bothered to learn our first official language and they didn't even appreciate the irony of his statement.

CHAPTER 21

SPREADING THE GOSPEL

In 1975, the training camps at Gormanstown, which had been so popular and which had spawned such a wave of energy, enthusiasm and expertise in hurling that had already set hearts and minds alight, were suddenly stopped.

The reasons given by the GAA were unclear. The one result of the success of the Gormanstown initiative was that coaching was now finally recognised by the GAA as a good thing. They scratched their heads and decided that it was something worthwhile and that it did work. The tidal wave set off by Gormanstown could not be ignored.

It could, however, be halted and controlled. And this is what happened, according to a number of people that I spoke to who all felt that its worth was never appreciated at a national council level. Having seen how brilliantly well the full immersion course such as those at Gormanstown worked, the GAA next decided to shut it down. In actual fact, the decision was taken to shut it down and then take the 'elements' from the Gormanstown experience and use them to create a different product.

This has resulted in some very worthy initiatives such as the 'Cúl 4 Kids' youth training camps and the weekend training courses that are carried out *in situ*. This latter idea is one which, it was thought, would allow coaches to hone their skills without having to travel. In other words, it would 'bring Gormanstown' to their door, thus allowing them to avoid the long journey and expense of a week away from home.

The trouble is that every person I spoke to that was involved in coaching does not agree with this idea. For them, there was no comparison with the Gormanstown camp. Perhaps the powers that be in the GAA looked up on Gormanstown as a bit of a holiday camp. This, after all, was a week that involved such non-Gaelic activities as golfing and swimming, where a growing, uncontrollable crowd gathered regularly and spent many evenings playing music and singing songs – a place where more socialising and frolicks went on than serious Gaelic sporting business. Perhaps it was something that the GAA feared was turning into a large benign monster that they couldn't control.

Justin McCarthy believes the latter: 'The GAA are often afraid of something or someone that will upstage them – that they can't control. I think that people in the organisation who make decisions like these are sometimes not hurling people – they are administrators, and I think that that's a fault within the system... It's all very well saying that this person or that person is a great coaching person, but those working within the GAA structure themselves are often interested in using that to make a job for themselves.'

My father's enthusiasm for developing the game was not dampened by such attitude. He was damned if he would let his love for the game and the truth be squashed by the higher powers in the GAA. As an aside, he took a similar attitude when it came to another important passion of his in life – namely the Catholic Church. I remember quizzing him once about how he could continue to support a church that had so much corruption and abuse of power at its heart, as I saw it. His answer was to say that all large organisations have an inevitable element of corruption within them, but that that was not going to deter him from following the path of truth. So off my father went on his righteous path to bring the truth, the passion, the enjoyment and the quest for knowledge to the people of Ireland.

My dad was, above all things, a GAA man. He was a hurling man first and foremost – of that, there's no doubt. Hurling was a game of many skills – skills that he, along with a few others, sat down and identified. Hurling was his first love, but he was a GAA man too and although his interest in Gaelic football was poor when compared with that of hurling, he did play football for Dungarvan and Affane and even played at inter-county level (in goals again!) for Waterford.

There aren't many photos of him playing football, but they do exist. He applied the same level of exactitude and precision when coaching football as he did when coaching hurling. Perhaps being a football coach is less complicated than being a hurling coach. I don't know and I can't tell for sure, but my father got results from his football coaching that, when applied, were just as impressive as those from his hurling coaching.

A testament to this is the fact that, under my father's influence, Tallow GAA had won every single county honour in football at all age levels with the sole exception of a senior title. It's true to say that on the hurling side the achievements were greater again, but then my father loved hurling much more than he loved the game of football.

By the mid-1980s, the spark had begun to fizzle out on the fortunes of Tallow GAA, for a number of reasons. One important factor was that the good years were marked by a particularly good crop of talent which was now getting on in years. Another, perhaps even more important, factor was the fact that the same person saying essentially the same things over and over again has only a limited life-span in terms of effectiveness. The attitude and line of patter of the best motivators in the world will inevitably become stale after a certain period of time and after a certain number of times repeated.

In the case of my father, the positive results were so dramatic that anyone who was watching could not fail to notice them. As the word had spread over the years, his name was legend as coach and motivator amongst many individuals. At Waterford county level, it was a different story. There was to be no offer to look after the fortunes of the county team – not yet, at least, and not on his own. But amongst the clubs, there was a strong appreciation in a far less politicised atmosphere.

This element of my father's hurling life (I hesitate to use the word 'career' as it does actually smack a little too much of professionalism) has turned out to be the most mysterious in many ways. It was a bit like being on the case of a master forger or something like that; trying to follow a trail around the country that no one person could outline for me clearly – not even my mother. Once, he was offered a sum of IR£100 per training session from a rival club in County Waterford. This was about 20 years ago, so the amount was considerable. But his response was to turn it down and to tell them that he really did not want to be a man who was available to the highest bidder. Moreover, he could not understand how anyone would do the sort of thing that he would do for financial gain. As far as he was concerned, to enter into such a world would be to dilute the entire reasoning behind the notion, to corrupt it.

So I had to try and retrace my father's footsteps, tracking down people who looked upon my dad as a demi-God, almost conjuring him up before my eyes as I spoke to them about how he changed their sporting fortunes and their lives. The list below, therefore, is only a sample, a taster of the many places he went to help out and of the sort of things he achieved and the impressions and legacies he left behind him.

1960s & '70s

These were the Gormanstown years and therefore a time when my dad was in regular contact with hurling people from all around the country – all hungry for to share and receive hurling knowledge. In the 1960s and the 1970s, my father had responded to many requests for assistance and coaching advice, particularly when they came from the more barren hurling spots of the country. Some of the most enthusiastic and committed hurling enclaves were to be found north of the border. The political tensions of the time did not defer him from his task. In fact, they only served to steel his resolve in bringing the 'Gospel' to the places that would have needed it most.

Like a sporting, socialist republican pastor with a passion for absorbing detail and passing it on in good spirit, my father always answered the distant call. Many of these people had come to know my dad through the Gormanstown coaching camps. Liam Hinphey – originally a native of the hurling county of Kilkenny but who for many years has been living in Co. Derry – was one such person: 'I met guys for years afterwards from fairly remote areas in the North who really didn't hurl much but they enjoyed Gormanstown and they all responded to your father... He had the "light touch", which is essential on these occasions. There was a Christy Ring Challenge in 1984 where they brought about 12 counties down to Cork to the school in Carrignavar. Ned took the Derry team. There was Henry Downey, Seamus Downey, Kieran McKeever – all those guys who were subsequently pretty prominent footballers. They came home absolutely delighted with the way the thing had worked out. The following year, Ned took them again and they loved his approach to the business. I think that that was Ned's great strength; he had a fairly light-hearted view. It wasn't the end of the world if you couldn't hurl, but it'd be a big help if you could!'

My dad was also to be big influence on a number of other clubs in Northern Ireland. In 1972, the Ulster Council of the GAA ran a coaching course at the New University of Ulster in Coleraine. Ned Power was selected as head coach. Liam Hinphey also remembers working alongside my father in 1969 in a coaching course in Orangefield in Belfast.

Castlelyons

Some time in the mid-1970s, my father went to this East Cork village – the birthplace of my mother – to help out with their fortunes. At the time, they were languishing in the lower B level.

'We couldn't hit the ball very far before he came,' remembers Michael Sheehan, who was involved with the club at the time. 'He got them to stop and think before they hit it as well.'

As well as raising the skills levels, Michael told me, he also got them to change the traditional attitude of over-physicality and to play cleanly: concentrating on and relying on only the skills. After a year or so with the club, he handed over the reins to Billy Sheehan.

The results were nothing short of dramatic: The club rose through the ranks of junior level unbeaten, before pulling off the same feat at intermediate level the following season to reach senior level in the shortest possible time-frame. It must be noted that this is all the more extraordinary an achievement when considering the fact that intermediate-level hurling in Cork is of a particularly high standard and with a lot of competition.

'It was on account of his coaching that we became senior,' says Michael. 'You couldn't believe how much we improved… We could hardly believe it ourselves!

'He couldn't stand any kind of dirty play – he was all about discipline and that was something we really needed. We used to have people training us up to that point who were all for "pulling hard on everything that moved"'.

'He changed all that and we became really clean… and we became a very popular team because of that, as well as a very successful one. We never got a player sent off after that.'

1980s

This is a period in which he was busy with Tallow. It was the club's most successful era at a senior level by far. But for most of that time, there were others running the teams and he helped out on a more intense level (such as when Tallow hurlers had progressed to the county final in 1984) only when he was called upon to do so.

Kerry

In 1981, Kerryman and a man who was to become president of the GAA Seán Kelly invited my father to assist with the development of hurling in his native county.

'I went for vice-chairman of the Kerry county board in 1981,' Seán told me over warm coffees on a cold wet midsummer's day in a Killarney hotel. 'Surprise, surprise… I got it. I was only a young lad at the time. As vice-chairman, I was given responsibility for hurling in Kerry.'

This responsibility was one that went with the position. It must be remembered that the county of Kerry is a predominantly football-playing one with a proud record of All-Ireland success. With 36 titles, it is considerably more than any other county in the country. Someone who is given the responsibility of developing hurling in Kerry, therefore, is given a job that would tend to be looked upon by the average full-blooded Kerryman as a bit of a poisoned chalice.

Seán, however, took a different approach: 'I decided that I'd do a bit more and I decided that I'd start hurling here in Killarney, in my home place. I thought that there wouldn't be much point in getting involved in hurling if I didn't do it in my own place.

'We got some hurleys together and got a few young lads playing and then we decided that we needed proper coaching. After making enquiries, Ned was one of the ones recommended to us.

'He responded immediately and with delight – he couldn't have been more helpful. He said that it was great to see us at hurling and wouldn't take a bob for it. He was absolutely marvellous: It was like Santy with all the kids around him. I think he was the finest coach you ever saw in terms of being able to relate to young people.'

The idea was to start from the ground up and get large groups of young people involved in hurling, but with my father's help, they succeeded in establishing themselves at senior level too. Seán himself was a member of that team, a Kerryman raised on football playing hurling and enjoying it for the first time in his life: 'One of the first times

I was playing was up in the stadium here. I went into goals and tried to puck out the ball and I missed it every time. I was about 28 at the time. I was so embarrassed. I heard him saying to one of the lads that the best way to learn hurling was to go into a handball alley and hit it against the wall. So I did, and I loved it. I was chairman of the East Kerry board and through that I was able to get seven-a-side hurling tournaments going. Then we got a senior team going out of that.'

The club – St Patrick's East Kerry – is still going strong today, having secured a county intermediate title during the time that my father was brought on board to apply some of his coaching know-how and his presence as an All-Ireland star.

Seán was president of the GAA from 2003 to 2006 – the first Kerryman to hold the honour. One of his initiatives as president was to introduce annual awards known as 'The President's Awards'. My dad was to receive a President's Award in 2006.

'Your dad was given the award because of his contribution to the GAA as a player, as a teacher and, above all, as a coach. Those awards were for people, like your father, who did everything on a voluntary basis.'

Seán told me again what a 'superb communicator' my father was and he compared him, in this sense, to the late writer Bryan MacMahon. 'Bryan was a teacher too and he also had that wonderful gift of being able to get down to the level of kids but at the same time remain slightly above them, so they were in awe of him but they weren't afraid of him, and he was able to bring every story he had down to their level and communicate it.

'Your father was the same way as a coach; he was able to get down to their level, and no matter how bad a fella was, he'd encourage them. He was one of those few people that others tend to gravitate towards… He had such a wonderful way about him, he was so mild… it was almost religious; that you listened and everything he said made sense.'

Ardmore

Along with Justin McCarthy and Peter Power, my dad did a two-week skills coaching course that covered all age levels in Ardmore. It's a small seaside village in a beautiful location with an ancient monastic settlement. We spent many family holidays there in a caravan park amongst a mobile population with a very high proportion of Cork people. This was around 1980 and the club (St Declan's), up to that point, had been solely a football club with very few real hurlers in the village and surrounds.

This course changed everything, as St Declan's GAA stalwart Billy Harty explained to me. 'Their enthusiasm alone was infectious and it's a period that we still refer to them as the founders of hurling in this football stronghold.'

The club started from scratch, in the Tallow mould, and have been playing at senior level for most of the last 10 years. At the time of writing, they have three representatives on the senior Waterford team – a proportionately high number for the size of the village.

Kilrossanty

Closer to home, Dad was asked to coach the Kilrossanty senior Gaelic football team. It was a small club based in a typically small rural setting, unaccustomed to success at county level over the previous two decades. In other words, it was ripe ground for the coaching techniques of my father. My father's people came from this rural part of East Waterford and, as Pa Walsh of Kilrossanty GAA said, 'He had a soft spot for us on account of his family coming from the area.' So it was a challenge and a request that he was very unlikely to refuse.

'I used to work with Eircom at the time,' said Pa Walsh, 'and I used to call to the school to your father and we used to have the chat about football. We were in the semi-final of the senior championship in 1983 and we beat Ferrybank. I met Ned after the match and I knew that we needed to get in somebody in the line of a top-class coach for the final. He just said to me: "Look Pa, you're in with a great shout." But I said that we needed someone to guide us. So I said is there any chance you might come down for a night. So he said "Call in to me some day you're in Tallow and I'll go down and have a look." And that's how it started.

'Myself and my brother were the two oldest on the team – I was 38 and he was 40. 'Twas a powerful team and Ned guided us. We won five senior championships in six years. We won it in '83, '85, '86, '88 and '89. We had fabulous days! Gee, we had great days! He was a top-class coach.'

Having arrived on the scene when Kilrossanty had already made it to a county semi-final without his help, I wondered if it was my father who had made the difference.

'He was the difference between winning and losing,' said Pa emphatically. 'We even won the under-21 title the same year, making the double. Just to listen to him alone… He made men believe in themselves.' In 1988, the club went further again, making it to the final of the Munster Club championship against the might of the famous Cork-city footballing club Nemo Rangers.

'Their greatest achievement,' said Pa, 'would have been the 1988 Munster club final against Nemo Rangers. Nemo had so many big guns playing with them; fellas that had been after winning five All-Ireland medals. But Ned felt that we couldn't believe that we could do it. In fact, there's no doubt about it but that we should have won it. It was all down to belief. It's a pity because it would have been the icing on the cake. The lads were mad about him.

'One thing about him is that he was so calm in his approach. Certain coaches would be excitable, we'll say at half time. They'd get all hot and bothered. But Ned would make us sit down, just relax. Then nice and gently, he would talk about it and he had a way with players that had them believing in themselves that… what way would I put it?... when he was finished having the chat with them, he had them in a way that nobody could beat them. Even in an ordinary player, he had them in a way that he felt he was as good if not better than his opponent.'

Seamus O'Brien, who had been a Waterford selector in the 1950s, also spoke of my father's unusually calm approach to coaching: 'His style of motivation was different – very different. He wasn't a man for banging his hurley on the table and shouting this and that. He was very moderate in what he said and he usually didn't speak until half time, so that he'd see how the team would perform in the first half.'

Youghal

The county Cork seaside town of Youghal is only 18 km or so from Tallow. In 1984, my dad was invited to coach their senior hurling team. They were beaten at the quarter-final stage of the Cork county championship but, as Youghal club man John Parker told me, it was 'anything but a failure, as Ned introduced our players and coaches to a training system and approach which were light years ahead of anything we had previously seen. This exposure to best practice of the day proved of enormous benefit to all players and teams in our club for many years. Ned passed on his knowledge in a very open way, to benefit our club and promote his beloved game of hurling generally. He had the gift of teaching the skills of the game in what appeared a simple way, but in reality, was the product of a lifetime devoted to it. He was a thorough gentleman and always sought to encourage a dedicated but sporting approach with no tolerance of foul play. Due to his many other commitments, his stay with us was all too short, but he left a legacy which has endured right to the present day.'

*   *   *

There's one story that my dad told us which sums a lot of what he was about as a coach: At one time during the early 1980s, my father was asked to help an unnamed club, one of the many whose call for assistance he would have answered. He duly arrived one October evening in the middle of a training session. As the team were put through their paces, my dad stood on the sideline and observed them as they engaged in a series of heavy exercises – sprinting, jogging, running, carrying one another on their backs, sweating and panting as they went back and forth before his eyes.

When they were finished, he pulled the trainer aside and, before the physically tired and aching panel assembled before him, he said:

'Lads, if you don't mind me asking…. What are ye doing here tonight?'

Everyone paused for a minute before somebody said:

'We're training.'

'Training for what?'

They all looked at one another with bewildered faces, wondering where this man was going with his puzzling series of questions.

'Well… for the match, for hurling.'

'Oh, I see,' said my father. 'I thought it might have been for the Grand National.'

CHAPTER 22

MY FATHER, THE B&B HOST

My dad retired in 1990 as a teacher, having worked his full 40 years. Looking back at his photos, he was a very healthy and youthful-looking 60-year-old. He looked ten years younger than his age, in fact.

For a man who had always been so active, I'm not sure that early retirement was something that agreed with him entirely. It's also quite a shock to the system when you've been working at the very same job for 40 years and then you suddenly stop. Or perhaps it was just a case of unfortunate luck that, almost as soon as he had gone into retirement, he was beset by a whole platoon of illnesses, each one lining up to have a go at him when the other had been dealt with, so that within ten years of his retirement, he had begun to look his age again, and even older.

A project that began when he retired from teaching was a major refurbishment of the house. Under the direction mostly of my mother, the family home (the nest from which all of us birds had now flown, except for my youngest brother Barry) was transformed from a four-bedroom bungalow into a seven-bedroom two-storey Chapel Street villa. It had become a Bed & Breakfast.

Coming home to the extended house was quite a treat for us who were living away from home. We came back to an altogether brighter and more modern version of what we had grown up with.

Mam and Dad only stuck to certain months of the year with their B&B business, which they ran from around 1994 to 2002. They must have done a good job between the pair of them because the guest book is full of extremely kind comments from impressed guests. The book doesn't start at the very beginning. They had been trading for an undetermined period of time (probably about a year) before my younger brother Éamonn decided that they needed a guest book and presented it to them one Christmas. There are many references in it to the charm of the hosts, the seemingly infinite quantity of toast available and the overall very satisfactory service that guests received.

One American guest from South Carolina who stayed in July 1995 wrote:

> *You were our first experience of Irish warmth and hospitality. What warm memories you've given us… so generous & attentive to our every need. Thank you for it all – especially Gretta's soda bread & Ned's daily promising weather forecasts!*

Another Dutch guest writes:

> *In spite of, or thanks to the graves next door, we could sleep like roses. Thank you for your real hospitality and the great Irish breakfast (and all the details about hurling).*

One Italian guest from 1997 clearly didn't quite get my father's explanation of the ancient Irish game:

> *Lovely service. Very kind people, thank you. Very good player hockey.*

In July 1998, a cyclist from Berlin writes:

> *Irish people very nice, but the Powers are the best in Ireland!*

'When a visitor would arrive at the house, it would take no longer than ten minutes before Ned would have the conversation steered round to games and hurling,' says my mother. I can certainly imagine that. For me, growing up with hurling in the house made it all a little boring from my perspective. I would often cringe and/or roll my eyes when I might bring a friend home as an adult and he would proceed to talk hurling with them. But my dad ate, drank and slept the sport so it never became boring for him and everyone ended up being charmed by his entertaining style of storytelling. He told hundreds of stories to entertain people and all were based on hurling or football games.

In many ways, my dad was well suited to the life of a B&B owner. When at home, my father was very often a quiet and private person; immersed in his own routines and thoughts, he was frequently non-communicative. One of my brothers (it's Éamonn, in fact) has been quoted as saying that 'if there were papers and food on the moon, he'd live there', summing up the basic requirements of 'home' Dad. But once in the company of others, he would become far more gregarious and he cranked up his public persona to the full. He was always full of chat and curiosity and was amusing company.

He was, in that sense, a candidate picked from a Bord Fáilte brochure. My mother says that they loved looking after their guests and were curious to meet them and find out about them. They also took the attitude of giving people plenty to eat for their breakfast: better to give a little too much than too little (hence, all the comments on the quantity of toast) and they would do their utmost to cook things to how the guest wanted it. My mother remembers one British guest who, when offered scrambled eggs, initially said no. He said that all the scrambled eggs he had encountered so far in Ireland had been 'too runny' for his taste. My mother persuaded him to try her scrambled eggs, assuring him that they wouldn't be runny. So, she made him the scrambled eggs without milk and with a little bit of effort and care. He left a happy tourist full of scrambled eggs *à la Maison Power*.

One interesting guest was the writer/lecturer and senator (and self-confessed Tallow native) Eoghan Harris. Having returned to his native place in May 2002, he wrote in the guest book:

Good bed, black toast, good conversation – fit for Raifteirí an File!*

The fact that the toast was blackened wasn't any black mark on the performance of the kitchen, for as my mother explained to me, the vociferous senator had requested his toast to be burned just as he liked it. It required more than two visits to the toaster, but inevitably he too left a happy customer.

A typical scenario during the B&B days, my mother told me, would be for my father to get so involved in his chat with guests that it would impinge on the important time schedule: The guests were to be out by midday so that the beds could be made up before it was swiftly followed by dinner preparation. My dad was certainly far from a tyrant around the house, but he did like to have his dinner on time. Please.

So, often my mother would be on her way to the dining room at 11:55 to ensure that the guests had finished their breakfast and were preparing to vacate their rooms only to find her husband and B&B partner standing before said guests, hurley held aloft, regaling them with another story of action on the GAA field.

It just wasn't an option for any of the guests to slip away quietly. Like the quantities of toast, it was probably better to have them leaving with a little too much entertainment than too little.

CHAPTER 23

RETIREMENT?

After 40 years of teaching, my father retired in June of 1990. Ireland had seen much change since he first come to Tallow. It was the year of Italia '90 and a pivotal time in Ireland's economic fortunes. The Berlin Wall had fallen and the Iron Curtain had been raised to reveal a whole host of countries that we never even knew existed before then and we watched them all emerge confused and blinking into the sunlight after having spent 40+ years in a state of virtual darkness.

Here in Ireland, there was to be a new-found confidence growing amongst Irish people as a population that had always been enterprising and resourceful began to gradually find its efforts being rewarded. From here on in, Ireland's economic data was to get better rather than worse. Within a short few years of this point, our traditional outward tide of emigration was to make an historical change to the totally unchartered territory of immigration.

Being somewhat out of step with trends as I tend to be, I actually emigrated as far as London that year, arriving in a country entering economic doldrums and a city that I could see beginning to empty itself of its huge Irish population.

So I missed out on seeing the big retirement 'do' in the school for my father. It was not the school he had started out in: The girls' and boys' schools had amalgamated ten years previously into one large modern mixed school that I had had the pleasure of attending for my last year of primary education. Although most of the teachers seemed to prefer the old boys' school, I preferred the new one: It was impressively large, it had exciting new things in it like gym equipment (not that it got much of a look-in in a PE regime that was dominated by hurling) and, of course, it had girls.

The send-off for my dad was a big affair. All the relevant dignitaries were there from the school board of management, as well as my mother and my brothers and sisters. A cake bearing the blue and white colours and in the shape of a hurley was presented to my dad. The girls cried and the boys looked on quietly as a much-loved hurling-obsessed educator took his leave of them and of the school building for the last time in his life.

Tallow GAA had been secretly organising an even bigger event for Dad. They wanted to show some appreciation in the year of his retirement for all that he had done for the club but they knew that he would refuse such fussing over him if he knew the extent to which they had gone.

My father was simply told that there was to be a formal presentation in the Community Hall, but what was organised was a bit more than that. The format was of the *This is Your Life* variety, complete with whole host of surprise guests. There were former comrades from the Waterford team of three decades previous – most of whom who had met up only the year before for the 30th anniversary of their All-Ireland heroics. In addition, there were many other friends from his hurling days with whom and against whom he had played and shared skills with at Gormanston. From Tallow GAA, there was a huge representation of members and players past and present. Seán was also based abroad at the time, so we were both flown home in secret and were produced at the appropriate hour by the MC for the night, who was none other than RTÉ's Micheál Ó Muircheartaigh.

If that level of logistical preparation had been known to him beforehand, he would have tried to stop it or tone it down or maybe he wouldn't even have turned up. But he was thrilled with the whole thing. It was a big night of celebration and a unique occasion for him to get fussed over in a spectacular way, as well as being able to catch up with family and friends. Such a gathering in honour of one person normally only happens at your wedding or at your funeral, so he was fortunate and he appreciated his great fortune.

Unsurprisingly, it was to be a busy enough retirement once the dust had settled. At the time of his entering the ranks of the 'third age', my youngest brother Barry was 11 years old and Dad's retirement coincided with him getting more and more involved in under-age hurling at Tallow GAA Club.

I took a very early retirement from hurling at around age 14. Éamonn played up to senior level with Tallow and he later played at junior level with Na Piarsaigh in Limerick. Seán played at junior and under-21 level and my youngest brother Barry carried on the hurling tradition for the longest period of all the sons. At the time of writing, he's still playing at senior level for Tallow. He's a goalkeeper, just like his father was. When Dad started coaching the younger players over the early 1990s, Barry was part of the set-up at this point and there were a number of players at the same level, some of whom went on to play for the senior Waterford team. This batch of talent included James Murray and Paul O'Brien. Incidentally, O'Brien was on the Waterford senior team in 2004 and he scored the winning goal in the semi-final against Tipperary. It was a sweetly struck first-time pull on the ground that whizzed through the air and ended up in the back of the net in dramatic fashion. For my father, that goal epitomised everything that he strove to encourage and achieve when coaching players of all ages and he was thrilled to the point of tears when his pupil made the right decision at the right time that resulted in such a fantastic result for Waterford, who were on their way to their second Munster championship in three years. Of that moment when he decided to make that winning strike by hitting it first time, Paul is quoted as saying: 'If I didn't hit it on the ground, Mr Power would have killed me!'

The underage group that my father was dealing with and which included Barry, stayed pretty much together through the levels, playing and perfecting their skills under the tutelage of the sixty-something maestro. This culminated in a minor County title for Tallow in 1997. It was their first in ten years and many of the players on the team were the sons of the successful senior teams of the early 1980s.

In between times, my father was still helping out with coaching the Tallow senior team. He was never in charge of the team during this period but was always involved around the fringes at least and he was still involved as late as 2003, when Barry made his senior debut. In 1991, he went back to a place he thought he'd never go to again – coaching with the senior Waterford side. I'm not sure what tempted him to do so, having had his fingers burned on the previous occasion. Perhaps he just couldn't resist such an opportunity. Just as in 1982–83, he went in as a package with Joe McGrath. Although the partnership was again short-lived, it was not entirely without success. This was the year before the breakthrough of the under-21 All-Ireland victory and things were still at a low enough ebb. Standards were raised, however and they managed victories against both Cork and Kilkenny that year. Although in each case, they were League matches (as opposed to the more testing championship games), they were noteworthy wins nonetheless on the road that would eventually lead to the re-establishment of Waterford's place at the top table of the national hurling scene. In fact, in the championship that year, Waterford went down against Cork, but the margin was tight (three points), a lot tighter than in their heavy losses to Cork and Tipperary in the championship campaigns of the two previous years.

Some aspects of the county set-up were slow to change: That season marked the very tentative beginnings of commercial sponsorship. My father and Joe asked the county board to provide two hurlies for each senior player and one hurley for each member of the intermediate team. They refused this modest expense. Not to be outdone by such a short-sighted approach, they approached Waterford Foods (now absorbed into the larger Glanbia group) for sponsorship of the cost of the hurlies. Waterford Foods were happy to do this but the county board still didn't consider it a good idea and, incredibly, permission for this deal was refused.

Apart from the hurling, in which he tinkered more than anything else (or, at least compared with the more full-on commitment of earlier years), Dad was also kept busy with his much-loved activities of golfing and reading the paper. It must be pointed out that his voracious reading of the papers not only kept him informed of the world at large, but he also used it to educate himself in the English language. He always had a habit of underlining every word that he couldn't understand and then consulting the word in the dictionary afterwards. This was a habit that stayed with him until the end.

He gave a lot of grinds in Irish to Leaving Cert students. As a teacher, he had taught Irish as well as he could, setting standards that few in the primary education system outside of Gaelscoileanna and Gaeltacht areas would follow. It was a constant bugbear of his that general standards of Irish amongst teachers in both national and secondary schools were so poor and he would never refuse to help, to answer the call of a student or his/her parents.

The Bed & Breakfast business that the family home became from about 1994 onwards was also something that occupied my parents' energies, particularly after my mother joined my dad in retirement in 1997. It was something that they both enjoyed, learning as they went along on a merry journey of chats, making beds, toasting bread and frying sausages.

My parents still went on holiday to France whenever they could and it was here that Dad had finally laid his Pioneer pledge to rest after many decades of total abstinence from alcohol.

Retirement meant that he had more time for golf. His regular spot was, of course, the local course at Lismore (from where ideally he would finish a round and then be home in time for dinner at one o'clock), but his two favourite places to play golf were Killarney and Lahinch, with a special leaning towards Killarney. Similar to hurling, my father never missed an opportunity to analyse and give coaching advice and many rounds of golf were punctuated with softly spoken but insistent words of advice, such as 'Follow through on it' or 'Up to your shoulder'. He didn't dispense such advice to everybody who played with him, of course. In fact, he was always a good judge of how receptive a person might be to receiving coaching and would give when it was needed and when the person had in interest in hearing it. His golfing was something that kept him fit in retirement and better able to face the illnesses that tormented him as he got older and he played a full 18 holes right up until about two years before his death. His last ever game of golf was in Killarney, when he played with my sister Patricia and with my brothers Barry and Éamonn, before a bout of pneumonia put a stop to his golfing days.

But hurling had a way of working its way back into his life at any given moment. He still got the calls for help and he still answered them. Tony Mansfield maintained that his major forte – and one for which he was never fully utilised – was as an individual skills coach.

Waterford and Tallow defender James Murray, like most Tallow youngsters, was coached by Ned Power and my dad had a strong personal involvement with his career right the way through it. For the U-14 All-Ireland Skills Competition of 1993, my dad gave James a lot of individual coaching. He achieved second place in the country. In the 2004 competition, Tallow had another strong entry in the young Thomas Ryan. My father worked with Thomas on refining his skills, night after night – quite literally – until he was well prepared. This time, he went one better than James Murray's achievement 11 years earlier and he won the All-Ireland title.

In March 2002, Dad was presented with a Hall of Fame Award at the WLR fm Lawlors Hotel 2001 GAA Awards ceremony in Dungarvan. The then Taoiseach Bertie Ahern officiated at event and my father told reporters that he was humble to receive the award, that the fact that he was being honoured as a former player made it all the more satisfying and that he especially enjoyed gatherings where GAA enthusiasts could meet up.

On the 1st of April 2006, my father was presented with a President's Award at Croke Park. This was a big black-tie affair. The whole family attended and we stayed overnight at the Croke Park Hotel. The awards had been established at the instigation of the then GAA president Seán Kelly and were conceived to honour voluntary contributions such as the work of my father. It was a great honour and a great night to be present – one of the truly big nights of his life.

Up until about 2005, my dad still worked with coaching under-age children. His contribution was recognised by the establishment of a Waterford-wide county under-age schools competition that was christened the Éamonn de Paor Medal. The inaugural competition was won by Knockanore Primary School. My nephew and my sister Patricia's son Edward Lonergan happened to be captain of the winning side and Dad found himself in the fortunate position of being alive and well to present the first Éamonn de Paor medal – named in his honour – to his own grandson in 2004.

CHAPTER 24

WHAT WAS IT ALL ABOUT?

My dad bore his illness with dignity and without complaint, except when it became really something to complain about. An initial analysis gave him about 12 years to live but he doubled that figure. There was a point when he was told that he might have six months to live. He lived another two years. The last time a doctor wrote him off was when he had been hospitalised after contracting pneumonia in late 2006. The sentence then was 'weeks, not months', but he was to defy that one too and he kept going for another year and a bit. I often think that maybe if he got just one more inaccurate prediction on his life expectancy, he would have lasted a bit longer through sheer determination. It wouldn't have surprised us because it was in his nature to be competitive and to strive to deny expectations.

He had a boundless energy and an appetite for life that kept him and everyone else around him going. He was the driving force behind the complete transformation of Tallow's sporting fortunes, having the leading role equally in raising funds to purchase a field for the club by tirelessly tracking down and then writing to every single individual that ever lived who had any sort of connection with Tallow and who might, therefore, have an interest in seeing the project succeed.

It's not easy to encapsulate and put into words what he meant to me, what he meant to my mother and my brothers and sisters and to everyone else whose lives he touched; to try and say just what he was. He was my father and that makes it difficult to stand back and say what else he was with any accuracy or even authority. In terms of his hurling persona, he was something of a diamond in the rough. In saying that, I mean that he was a hurling man that came out of a family with no hurling or sporting prowess to speak of. It was because of this, I believe, that he never placed any burden of expectation on the shoulders of his sons in terms of following his lead in hurling. Any sense of expectation would come from others, from people who might have expected a son of Ned Power to be a keen hurler or a daughter or Ned Power to be a keen camogie player. He just happened to have a strong interest in sport and an unquenchable thirst to learn more about it and to play it to the absolute best of his ability. That thirst and drive propelled him along a path that would take him to places and to heights that seem extraordinary looking from the sideline.

But to my father, there was nothing terribly extraordinary about it all because he was always looking forward to the next thing, not looking behind to see what he had done. He was satisfied only in moments and he got a kick out of it when he would achieve a target such as the Intermediate county title for Tallow in 1974 or witnessing the winning goal by Paul O'Brien in the 2004 Munster semi-final – a tangible fruit as a result of efforts made striving to reach perfection over time.

One of my dad's old friends Joe McGrath spoke to me of a hierarchy of elements of his life that were important to him. In ascending order or importance, Joe listed these five fundamentals: Play; Work; Country; Family; God. These were basics aspects of Joe's life that he had prioritised over the years, but from the many conversations that the two men had together, he felt that it was certainly a very similar approach to life for my father.

You might call it the structure of a moral code or simply the crystallisation of life experience into something tangible, something that you can list and lay out in clear terms. Whatever it is, it could easily be applied to my dad's life. His own code by which he lived his life can be sketched out in a similar fashion.

For example, he was passionate about hurling and GAA (play) when he was doing it, but equally, he knew that it was just a game; something at the end of which you shake hands and part on good terms and it was not as important as your work, your country or your family. And nothing was as important as God.

He had a powerful faith which dictated the manner in which he approached everything else in life. He wasn't a lackey to the often overbearing power of the Catholic Church in Ireland but he gave it the respect he felt it deserved. He was a believer in the power of example rather than in the power of preaching. Any 'bad eggs' in the Church were to be expected, as they were to be expected in any large organisation, and he was damned if they were going to put him off his solid beliefs and his devotion to the sacraments. In any case, any serious row with members of the clergy (or with anyone else for that matter) was to be quickly forgotten and made up with a warm, firm handshake – just like you do at the end of a match. In the end, there's only one place you're going and you're a fool if you're not ready for that.

It was very wet on the day that he was buried. There were a lot of people at the funeral. Nobody was counting so it's impossible to say how many were there. There was a guard of honour from Tallow GAA and one from Cois Bríde – the joint Tallow/Shamrocks club. The day before, people had come to pay their respects at the family home. There was a non-stop queue outside the house from the morning until well after dark. In an earlier existence, I worked in a funeral home and was acquainted with the entire procedure of preparation in a manner that lent the whole of the proceedings an even more surreal ambience.

The crowds kept filing through and every once in a while a familiar face from previous years would emerge like spirits out of a gloom of confusion. Wakes are bizarre events at the best of times. Everyone is gathering for a solemn event but the size of the crowd and general chatter makes it feel more like a party atmosphere. You find yourself joking and laughing with people while beside you the corpse of your father is lying silently and you're just not sure how you should feel about it all.

You laugh to keep away the tears and you wonder what sort of person you are to be laughing at such an occasion. Yet here they all are – people who came from far and wide to say goodbye. A lot of people kiss the body goodbye but I didn't do it. I made a firm semi-subconscious decision not to do it, I think, long before my father died. I'm not sure whether it was because I didn't want to say goodbye to him or whether I just didn't want to say goodbye in that way. We all try to keep it going but there's no getting away from the truth itself and it was by the graveside that I finally dissolved into sobs. Lots of people were there too.

I shook hands and tried my best to remember as many faces and names as I could but I actually could not remember many of them and I have since met a lot of people that I cannot clearly remember meeting at the funeral, which is the exact opposite of what is supposed to happen, according to what I heard beforehand.

I often think of him as a socialist. Not a red-beret wearing, placard-waving middle-class socialist, but a real one and a Catholic one: someone who was always willing to give and share with his fellow human beings as much as was humanly possible in order to improve their lot and to improve the lot of society in general, and always with a joke and a positive outlook on the situation at hand, and always trusting that it would work out all right in the end.

He was like that with his brothers and sisters as a youth in Dungarvan. He was like that with his team-mates when he played with winning county teams. He was like that with a number of the more unfortunate members of society – giving a helping hand to people that everyone else would stay clear of, learning as much as he could and then enthusiastically sharing his knowledge of what he'd learned with everyone, even those on the opposition in a match. He was part of a revolution in coaching that started as his ten-year inter-county career was ending and he brought that revolution to everyone who wanted to hear it.

He was a husband to Gretta and a father to Patricia, Seán, Annette, me, Éamonn and Barry. That was my father, the hurling revolutionary.

---

[1] *Traditional Irish politics is not divided between left and right but on whether or not you agreed with the Treaty of December 1921, which effectively divided Ireland into the Republic of Ireland and Northern Ireland. The republican side argued against accepting the Treaty and for a continuation of striving to achieve an all-Ireland independent republic.*

* *'I only have one wife/ban.'*

* *A reference to the famous nineteenth-century Irish poet Antoine Ó Raifteirí*

INDEX

ABOUT THE AUTHOR

Conor Power is a journalist who contributes regularly to a number of national newspapers on a range of subjects, including travel, property and the arts. This is his first book.

He lives in West Cork with his wife Fiona and their three sons.